FOREWORD BY
TONY DUNGY

THE JERSEY EFFECT

BEYOND THE WORLD CHAMPIONSHIP RING

HUNTER SMITH
& DARRIN GRAY
with Stephen Copeland
& Ken Turner

THE JERSEY EFFECT

DARRIN GRAY AND HUNTER SMITH

WESTBOW
PRESS
A DIVISION OF THOMAS NELSON

WestBow Press books may be ordered through booksellers or by contacting:

WestBow Press
A Division of Thomas Nelson
1663 Liberty Drive
Bloomington, IN 47403
www.westbowpress.com
1-(866) 928-1240

Because of the dynamic nature of the Internet, any web addresses or links contained in this book may have changed since publication and may no longer be valid. The views expressed in this work are solely those of the author and do not necessarily reflect the views of the publisher, and the publisher hereby disclaims any responsibility for them.

ISBN: 978-1-4497-3273-8 (sc)
ISBN: 978-1-4497-3274-5 (e)

Library of Congress Control Number: 2012900957

Photos in The Jersey Effect were taken by AJ Macht or Don Larson and were graciously provided by our friends at the Indianapolis Colts.

Printed in the United States of America

WestBow Press rev. date: 5/14/2012

FOREWORD

"Football builds character." We hear that phrase so often that we take its truth for granted, without stopping to consider what is really being said. Football is the most popular sport in America today, and its players are publicized, and often idolized, to an unbelievable level. Our boys grow up wanting to play football. They are drawn by the excitement and the adrenaline rush the game provides. And we, as parents, want them to play football. Why? We are drawn in by the excitement as well but often fall back on that axiom that participating in team sports builds character. And we view football as the ultimate team sport. If they play football, our boys will become physically and mentally tough! They'll learn how to work together for a common goal and how to overcome tough losses and keep pushing toward that goal. We encourage our boys to sign up for the pee-wee football team because surely these lessons are all things that will benefit them later on in life. After all, football builds character, doesn't it?

I think we really need to examine that statement and not just accept it as gospel. If football really builds character, then the longer you play and the higher up the football ladder you go, the more it should benefit you. It would make sense, then, that players who make it to the NFL level and have a long professional career would reap the most benefits from the sport and have the most successful lives after football. But that's not the story the facts tell. When you look behind the scenes, it appears that the higher up you go in the game, the more problems you have.

In major college football, it seems that every day we're reading of eligibility issues, low graduation rates, and disciplinary problems.

On January 28, 2006, in an article titled "Life after the NFL: Typically a struggle," *USA Today* reported that, in fact, 78 percent of all NFL players are divorced, bankrupt, or unemployed two years after leaving the game. And NFL players are six times more likely to commit suicide, citing the work of Ken Ruettgers, former twelve-year veteran player with the Green Bay Packers and advocate for players transitioning from professional sports through his organization, GamesOver.org

What do these statistics mean? Do they mean that football is an inherently bad game and we shouldn't let our boys play, for fear that they'll end up an emotional wreck? No, I don't believe that at all. I played and coached football for most of my life, and I have a son playing college football now. What it does mean, however, is that football doesn't build character any more than factories build automobiles. Our character is shaped by the people we are around, by our experiences, and by our beliefs about why God put us here on earth. And depending on how it is taught, football can be either a positive enhancement or a destructive force in that development.

This impact of football on the lives of young men is what *The Jersey Effect* is all about. Hunter Smith knows this subject very well. He was an outstanding football player who enjoyed success at every level of the sport. Hunter played in a tremendous high school program in Sherman, Texas, and then went on to star at Notre Dame. He played twelve years in the NFL, punting for the Indianapolis Colts and Washington Redskins. For seven of those years, I had the pleasure of coaching him with the Colts, and I got to watch him grow not only as a player but also as a husband, as a father, and as a man. Hunter was able to navigate the emotional roller coaster of big-time football—from highs like winning a Super Bowl to lows like fumbling a snap that cost his team a chance at victory (and he truly grew from both). This book describes how he was able to do that and not get swallowed up by success or disappointment.

Photo courtesy of the Indianapolis Colts

It's my belief that young people involved in sports need to grow academically, athletically, socially, and spiritually. That should be the goal of parents, teachers, counselors, and coaches. Unfortunately, as a professional coach, I saw too many examples of young men who had developed athletically but hadn't grown in the other three areas. And that's what leads to the frightening statistics mentioned previously. *The Jersey Effect* speaks to parents about the importance of not neglecting our children's academic, social, and spiritual lives.

This book was also written with the young athlete in mind. Young men and women who are reaching for the stars are naturally driven. They thirst for the thrill and excitement of heated competition. They quest for the attainment of physical fitness and agility of mind when it comes to the sport of their choosing. And through it all, they need the love and guidance of parents, mentors, and coaches to avoid the pitfalls that often come when they strive to be the very best at what they set out to do. Just as important, or even more so, is the need to find and keep a fully engaged relationship with Jesus Christ.

The Jersey Effect deals with many of the dynamics and issues that our boys are facing today, whether they're athletes or not. Hunter Smith and coauthor Darrin Gray, who works with an organization called All Pro Dad, do a great job of mapping out the best way for boys to navigate that journey to manhood, one who starts with following the spiritual guidance of Jesus Christ.

Photo courtesy of the Indianapolis Colts

After Hunter's first son was born, he and I had a lot of conversations about parenting and fatherhood. Now that his son is getting to the point where he is interested in football, we've talked about youth leagues and what should be emphasized in youth coaching. I know this is a passion for him, and he wanted to share with people how he and some of his teammates got the most out of their experiences in the game. If you have a son who is interested in sports or you work with young people in any capacity, this book will help you look at the process a little differently and aid you in helping them build the character we want them all to possess.

Tony Dungy
Former head coach of the Super Bowl XLI
Champion Indianapolis Colts
NBC Sunday Night Football commentator
Author of the best-selling books *Quiet Strength*, *Uncommon*, and *The Mentor Leader*

TRIBUTE

COACH JOHN OUTLAW

As a young boy in the midsized "Friday night lights" football town of Sherman, Texas, it was always my dream to be a Bearcat. In many ways—and this is no exaggeration—this dream meant more than being a Texas Longhorn or even a Dallas Cowboy. The coach of the Sherman Bearcats played a large role in this. John Outlaw was a legend.

Wherever he coached, he won. Inside his leathery larger-than-life persona was a very sensitive and decent man. Coach Outlaw was one of my heroes. When I was fifteen years old, my dream of playing varsity became a reality. Coach Outlaw went from being a distant figurehead to being a coach and a mentor. And, as usual, we won.

In adult life, John became my friend. Several months ago, I interviewed him for *The Jersey Effect*. He was still doing what he loved. Coaching football. Even after all these years I heard the passion in his voice about the game, but even more, I heard a deeper sense of concern and care for the lives of the young men he was leading.

On December 23, 2011, just two months after we spoke, John passed away. When we last spoke, he put it all in perspective: "They ain't gonna put any of them wins in your casket." Those words, and the way he said them, will always ring true in my ears. Thanks, Coach Outlaw, for putting it all in proper perspective.

Hunter Smith

ENDORSEMENTS

Hunter Smith has the number one qualification to write this book: integrity. He experienced the glory of Notre Dame football and the game's ultimate prize, yet he defines success by another world's measure. He and his collaborator, Darrin Gray, use this book to share the same higher purpose with the next generation of athletes. If parents, coaches and players will heed this message, the games will be more fun, families will be strengthened, and life champions will be built.

> – Jay Hein: Former Director, White House Office of Faith Based and Community Initiatives

The Jersey Effect is a testament to what it means for an athlete to pursue the ultimate prize in life. Hunter Smith and other elite athletes use their platform to communicate meaning to life that goes far beyond the Super Bowl ring and World Champion status. It's a life-changing message that this generation needs to hear. I am eager to get this book into the hands of the thousands of young athletes and coaches who attend the National Association of Christian Athletes events and camps!

> – Dave Sekura: NACA National Director

For over two decades I have witnessed many families struggle with unhealthy attitudes about sports. The Jersey Effect provides parents with the real-world tools they need to teach their children about how to keep sports in a proper perspective. Hunter Smith and Darrin Gray clearly have their finger on the pulse of this important topic. The noteworthy stories in their book deliver enduring principles that clearly articulate the rights and responsibilities that every athlete must embrace in order to maximize their God-given potential.

– Mark Merrill: President of *Family First* and host of nationally syndicated radio program, *Family Minute with Mark Merrill*

This is a book every athlete, coach or person of influence needs to read. It addresses the dangers of wearing the jersey the wrong way and shines a spotlight on the power that the jersey wields when worn the right way. It's not just another fluffy, religious sports book. Hunter Smith and his teammates dig deep to teach important lessons about the jersey in a captivating way. Whether stories from the Colts on the 2006 Super Bowl team or anecdotes from Hunter's own life, it's an entertaining and convicting read.

– Robert Walker: Publisher of *Sports Spectrum* magazine

CONTENTS

REAL CHAMPION

A season so unlikely, a victory so unbelievable that it had to be … God.

Shaping, molding us in his image. This is the covenant that was made.

A joyful assembly—a small band of brothers, honorable men—

athletes, warriors, believers—grounded by their love for God and others.

A holy union. A relentless coming together for a common cause.

So many leaders willing to follow … a grand design.

A journey much longer and harder than expected.

Men perfectly equipped to produce something timeless and meaningful.

Paradigm change. A story rewritten. Deeper than imagined.

Lasting impressions. Influence 360 degrees.

God spoke. Humble men listened. Bright lights on a mountain.

Quiet locker room prayers heard around the world.

Salty, enough to speak … truth and lies.

A cauldron of adversity, emptiness, and unspeakable joy.

Special moments never mentioned.

Bringing great glory to the ultimate Author and Creator.

Join the story. You likely already have. Remember winning and losing.

Always unfinished, time and time again, always complete.

DARRIN GRAY

SUPER BOWL XLI
CHAMPIONSHIP TEAM

Photo courtesy of the Indianapolis Colts

INTRODUCTION

From where I sit in my study, I can see many pictures.

There's one of an old F-16 with a Colts horseshoe painted on its tail taking its final flight. It was flying over Lucas Oil Stadium. The picture was given to me by the pilot and snapped by his wingman just a few yards away.

There is a panoramic of a kickoff at Notre Dame Stadium. I saw it at a memorabilia store years ago. When I got closer I noticed that Notre Dame was playing Michigan. The electric atmosphere almost jumped out of the frame. With an even closer look, I noticed that Notre Dame was kicking off. Closer, I realized that it was *me* kicking off. That seemed really cool, but I wasn't about to buy a piece of sports memorabilia. It's just not me. A few weeks later my father-in-law surprised me with it. It's been on my wall ever since.

There's a picture of our Super Bowl celebration. There's another with my Colts teammates and me standing on the steps of the White House with the president of the United States. There's even a Redskins team picture.

In many of the pictures are faces. Faces of men I played with early in my career long removed from the game of football. Men whose lives have been tragic tales told over time. It is only when you look deep into these photographs that you see the tragedies and their roots. They were affected by the jersey occasionally for better, but largely for worse.

It is for men and women, boys and girls, young and old, Colts fans and not, that I have partnered with Darrin Gray to write this book. Almost two years ago, Darrin and I began to reach out to former teammates and coaches of mine from the 2006 Indianapolis Colts Super

Photo courtesy of the Indianapolis Colts

Bowl championship season. The purpose of speaking with them was to find out how reaching the pinnacle of professional sports had affected their lives. Some of them were retired. Many were and are still playing. All of them are good friends of mine whom I trust implicitly. To put it bluntly, these guys are the "real deal." They are my brothers. Their transparency and willingness to open up about their struggles may shock you. But because of their honesty and vulnerability, this book has the potential to strengthen your faith, redefine your worldview, and help you recognize the negative and positive effects that a jersey can have.

Each chapter begins with a letter. The letters are authentic and written by my own hand. The purpose of these letters was to affirm and commend these men, but also to invite them to be a part of *The Jersey Effect*. (In the best interest of saving space, we chose to leave out the invitation part of each letter.) It's important to tell people how you feel while there is time. I am happy to have had the opportunity to express the brotherly love I feel for these men and include it in these pages.

Yes, this is a remembrance of the Tony Dungy era, the Peyton Manning era, and the Super Bowl XLI victory. This was the team you loved for a decade. This was an era that breathed life into Indianapolis and its fans—an era that has long passed with the many transitions of the 2011/12 season. As the featured players and coaches reminisce on the 2006 season—the defensive struggles, the doubts, the miracle run, the AFC Championship comeback against New England, and the hoisting of the Lombardi Trophy in a Miami downpour—you'll take a nostalgic step back into one of the most exciting years in Colts football. The structure of this book is what makes it compelling. But it's also more than that.

As the cover says, this book goes beyond the world championship. In our struggle to win a world championship, we learned so much about who we were as men. Our identity was refined and crystallized as we wrestled with our own ego and pride. It was as if we were on a journey from self to selflessness. This is a behind-the-scenes look at Colts football—a personal and intimate tale told to help you gain perspective about the truths and lies of this often manipulative world.

Photo courtesy of the Indianapolis Colts

The stories in this book create another picture. It is a picture of what to do and what not to do as an athlete and person. Whom to trust and whom not to trust. What to believe and what not to believe. I chose the men I did, not because they are perfect. I chose them because they have a proper perspective on athletics and this world in a generation of upside-down priorities. It is my and Darrin's hope that as you read these pages, you are challenged, stretched, realigned, and yes, even entertained. The jersey will affect all of our lives. We, as athletes at all levels of play, will in turn use the jersey to affect the world—for worse or for better.

What will your jersey effect be?

CHAPTER 1

HUNTER SMITH

THE SUPER BOWL: THE JOURNEY IS MORE IMPORTANT THAN THE PRIZE

Photo courtesy of the Indianapolis Colts

#17
Punter
Height: 6' 2"
Weight: 209
Age: 34
Born: August 9, 1977, Sherman, Texas
College: Notre Dame
Experience: 12 seasons (Colts 10, Redskins 2)
High School: Sherman High School,
Sherman, Texas

"Every man dies. Not every man really lives." –William Wallace.

I tried to deny the emptiness.

But when you achieve what you thought would satisfy you and it lets you down, there is a window into the soul.

That's what this book is—a window into the soul.

My Journey and the Colts' Journey

Of course, I'll never forget that February night in 2007. It was undoubtedly the epitome of my professional career—when we defeated the Chicago Bears 29–17 in Super Bowl XLI. After all, it'd been a long road for us Colts.

Sure, it was awesome to be a part of a team that accumulated 115 wins in a ten-year span, the most successful organizational decade in NFL history, but it took forever to win the big one, the Super Bowl. We were always in contention, but media and fans believed we'd continue to choke in the playoffs. A columnist even wrote an article profiling the monkey on Peyton's back. Ridiculous, yes. But there's no doubt, it was there.

The years leading up to our Super Bowl victory were frustrating enough. I can't imagine how it felt for the old-timer fans who routinely witnessed a team that, ahem, continually produced records comparable to that of the 2011/12 Colts, who were winless after fourteen weeks.

After years of success in Baltimore (winning three world championships, including a 1971 Super Bowl victory over the Dallas Cowboys), the Colts began looking for a new home. The stadium in Baltimore needed severe upgrades, and the franchise had fallen into serious decline. In 1981, the Colts were 2–14, and after the NFL strike in 1982, they went 0–8–1.

So in late March 1984, Mayor William Hudnut of Indianapolis and Colts owner Robert Irsay reached an agreement that triggered the Colts' sudden departure to Indianapolis. Secretly. Overnight. In Mayflower trucks. The official announcement was made on March 29.

There were many dismal seasons in Indianapolis following the big move. Maybe it was the ghost of Johnny Unitas. No one knows. But whatever the case, they were awful. In 1997, Jim Irsay was named the owner and CEO of the Colts, and Bill Polian became the president of the organization. Nothing really changed. Yet. After finishing 3–13 in 1997, Jim Mora replaced Lindy Infante as head coach, leading them to another 3–13 record in 1998 after acquiring rookie quarterback Peyton Manning from the University of Tennessee.

That brings us to 1999, the year I graduated from Notre Dame. I was recruited by Notre Dame legend Lou Holtz as a quarterback but became the starting punter my freshman year. That was frustrating, if I'm being honest. I wasn't doing what I loved to do—which was playing quarterback or receiver—and I was afraid I was going to get stuck punting the football for four years ... which is exactly what happened.

One day, Coach Holtz pulled me aside and said, "Hunter, you are going to be a punter in the NFL for ten years, and I'm not going to be responsible for playing you in another position and risk you getting injured." It was most prophetic

Photo courtesy of the Indianapolis Colts

because I was drafted by the Indianapolis Colts in 1999 and went on to have a twelve-year career in the NFL. I played in every game during my four years at Notre Dame, had the third most punts of any player in Notre Dame history (174), and recorded the second most yards per punt (41.2); my 79-yard punt against Arizona State was the longest by a Notre Dame punter since 1935. Coach Holtz wasn't even born the last time someone punted a ball that far ... and that's saying something. If I wanted to play another position, I wasn't making a very good case for it.

Although I've spent most of my life in Indiana—at Notre Dame, with the Colts, and at my current home in Zionsville, Indiana—my roots are actually in Texas. My high school coach's name was John Outlaw. Classic Texas. And no, he didn't walk around biting a toothpick, wearing a cowboy hat, and spinning a pistol in his fingers. Okay, maybe the toothpick.

I learned a lot from Coach Outlaw. The most memorable thing I recall him saying to me was, "They ain't gonna put any of them wins in your casket," which is a radical statement considering the NFL players he has coached (Bryan Gilmore, Terrence Kiel, Don Muhlbach, Rex Hadnot, and Dez Bryant) and the state championships he has won. Coach Outlaw said my most memorable game was the final contest of my senior year. I broke my hand in the first half but returned to play the remainder of the game, nearly leading us to victory in front of twenty-five thousand fans. So now you know: I wasn't always *just* a punter. I was actually an athlete in my former life. But it was punting that got me into the NFL. God has a funny way of working things out.

I played in all sixteen games my first year with the Colts and witnessed the team produce an NFL record ten-game turnaround for a stellar 13–3 record. Believe it or not, there was a time in Indianapolis when the city doubted the talents of Peyton Manning. Not anymore. The 1999 season silenced that.

In 2000, we finished 10–6 and lost to the Dolphins in the wild-card round. And in 2001, we staggered to a 6–10 record thanks to seven losses in our last nine games. Of course, there *was* one positive that came out of the season—the Jim Mora "playoffs" rant.

I played three seasons for Coach Mora. And we had one encounter I'll always remember. I was in the Colts' locker room my rookie season after practice, and someone had a rope for some reason. So I made a lasso out of it and started roping things (and maybe people, too). People assumed it was a trait I learned growing up on the one-thousand-acre cattle ranch in Texas. But I actually learned it at an Irish Catholic university when my friends and I started roping things in the dorm. Today, I'll go outside and rope my kids as they run around in our yard. (It's fun, okay? And it's a skill I don't want to lose.)

Anyway, I was focused on ropin' when Mora walked in. The locker room got quiet, but I didn't see him, so I just kept roping things. Then Mora spoke in his high-pitched, crusty voice, "Hey, you're pretty good at dat."

I looked at him, and we stood there awkwardly staring at one another.

"Here," he said quickly, holding up his arm. "Rope my arm."

I got nervous. What if I hit him? What if I missed? What if I accidently lassoed his head, the rope becoming a noose for my head coach?

I missed.

"Welp," Mora said, as if analyzing my roping skills. "Here, try again." And he once again held up his arm.

"Okay," I said.

"Nah, the hell with it," Mora interrupted. "You get one chance on the field. You get one chance to rope my arm." Then he walked away.

So yeah, that was the Mora era. He was fired later that year and replaced by Tampa Bay's Tony Dungy—a coach who radically changed the culture of the Indianapolis Colts. Tony led us to a solid 10–6 record in 2002 but an unfortunate 41–0 loss to the Jets in the wild-card round. In 2003, a rivalry began to form. We finished 12–4, spanked Denver 41–10 in the wild-card round, slipped by Kansas City 38–31 in the divisional round, but lost to the dreaded New England Patriots 24–14 at Gillette Stadium in the AFC Championship. The Pats also beat us 38–34 in the regular season at the RCA Dome and went on to win the Super Bowl 32–29 over the Carolina Panthers. That season may have been the birth of Indy's hatred for New England.

The 2004 season was practically identical to 2003. We finished 12–4, defeated Denver 49–24 in the wild-card round, and then lost to—you guessed it—New England, 20–3, on a snowy evening in Foxborough, our lowest point total since our season opener in 2003. And again, the Pats went on to win their second consecutive Super Bowl with a 24–21 victory against Philadelphia. And just to rub more salt in the wound (it gets better, I promise), New England had beaten us in the regular season as well, when we kicked off the NFL season with a Thursday night contest against the defending Super Bowl champions. We were trailing

27–17 after three quarters but couldn't complete our comeback, falling 27–24 in Foxborough (again) as our nemesis recorded its sixteenth consecutive victory. Those were some painful years for Colts fans and players—continually witnessing our archrival not only beating us but also going on to win Super Bowl championships. We were so close. But there was something about the playoffs. And there was something about New England.

If there was ever a year we were destined to win the Super Bowl, it was 2005. And everyone knew it. Looking back, that was clearly the best team I played on. We started off the season with thirteen straight victories, including a rewarding 40–21 victory at New England despite Peyton being 0–7 in Foxborough. Sure, they had some injuries. But it was still the Patriots. We lost two of our last three regular season games, but only because Tony rested our starters for the playoffs.

In week 16, we realized that our season had become something much more than simply winning. We had a reason to win … for Tony. That's because two days before our second to last regular season game, his eldest son, James Dungy, passed away. Our hearts ached for him. The season became bigger than wins and losses, bigger than the Patriots, bigger than ourselves. Our goal was clear: we were going to win a Super Bowl—not for us, not for the city, not for anyone else—but for Tony Dungy.

When the Patriots lost in the divisional round, it seemed even more apparent this was our year. We had a clear shot to the Super Bowl. It sounds ridiculous, but when a team knocks you out of the playoffs two consecutive years and goes on to win two Super Bowls, you can't help but think that way.

After a first-round bye, we faced No. 6 seeded Pittsburgh in the divisional playoff. The Steelers jumped to a 21–3 lead before we rallied in the final quarter to get within three points (21–18). Our kicker, Mike Vanderjagt, had a 46-yard field goal at the end of the game to tie it and complete a monumental comeback … but it turned out to be, well, let's just say not one of his better kicks.

I remember catching the snap, placing it, and being able to tell that

Mike made solid contact with his foot (as the holder, I could always tell if it was a strong kick). I slowly looked up at the uprights, believing the game was heading into overtime. Nothing. Next, I looked around me, suspecting that the kick had been blocked. Nothing. The football had seemingly vanished. And I finally spotted it soaring into the second row of the stands, severely wide of the uprights.

I couldn't believe it. Just like that, our Super Bowl dreams were over. Our hopes of bringing Tony a Super Bowl … over. The best team I'd ever been a part of—and we didn't even win a playoff game. We, the No. 1 seed, were stunned by Pittsburgh, the No. 6 seed, the only time that had ever happened in NFL history. A sports writer later joked that search-and-rescue teams were unable to find that football. Believe me; they're still looking for it.

The 2006 season didn't show nearly as much promise as 2005.

There were guys starting on the Colts who wouldn't have gotten signed on any other NFL team. Our defense was never stellar, but they were pitiful that year. Against Jacksonville, we surrendered *375 rushing yards*, the second-highest total in NFL history, Maurice Jones-Drew rushing for 166 yards and Fred Taylor going for 131. I'll say it again: *375 rushing yards*.

I vividly remember standing on the sidelines during a kickoff that game and hearing the public address announcer come over the stadium speakers: "If Maurice Jones-Drew runs this kickoff for a touchdown, some lucky Jaguar fan will win twenty thousand dollars!" Next thing I knew, Maurice sprinted right by me. All I did was turn my head. Then I hung my head. "Touchdown!"

We were last in the league that year in rushing defense, yielding 2,768 total yards and 5.3 yards per carry, and last in return defense, surrendering 2,029 yards and 26.0 per return. Overall, our defense ranked twenty-first in the league, giving up 332.3 yards per game.

Yes, we were still winning. We totaled twelve wins for the fourth time in four years (don't ask me how), won the AFC South for the fourth year in a row, and even won our first nine games. But we were going into the playoffs as a No. 3 seed, a seed that hasn't fared too well over the years (only the 1988 San Francisco 49ers have won a Super Bowl). And the truth is that the media and fans didn't care about winning in the regular season. We had proven we could do that the last half decade. Everyone, rather, was interested in one thing: the Super Bowl.

Another reason we were suboptimal was our core players. This is what I consider the archetype of a core player: your backup offensive lineman who is also on your frontline on field goal units and the kickoff return team, or your backup safeties, or your third-string running back. Core players are why the Patriots can still go 11–5 whenever Tom Brady goes down. Core players are also why the Colts nearly go winless when Peyton Manning goes down. Because the Colts don't have enough of them. The Patriots survived with Matt Cassel as their quarterback because the *team* was good. This Colts team in 2006—take my word for it—was not good … at all. The offense was rolling as usual, but the defense and special teams created significant insecurity and doubt regarding our chances of going all the way.

But that's also what made 2006 special. We created the right synergy to get the job done. We came together. And come playoff time—despite the critics of our defense and special teams—that's exactly what we did. In the AFC wild-card game against Kansas City, our defense silenced the skeptics by holding Larry Johnson to 32 yards on 13 carries. I remember Tony Dungy saying something ironic before the game. "We can stop the run," he encouraged us. "We may not hold Larry to 35 yards, but we can stop him." After the game, he joked, "I was right; we didn't hold Larry to 35 yards. We held him to 32." It was solely because of our defense, in fact, that we even won that game. Peyton threw a season-high three interceptions, two of which were to former New England player Ty Law (go figure), and all of our points in the first half came from the boot of Adam Vinatieri. We won 23–8.

Everyone thought our defensive performance that game was a fluke. So against the Ravens, our first playoff return to Baltimore since the great *Mayflower* voyage, we proved that it wasn't, holding the Ravens to 83 total rushing yards. Peyton struggled again, passing for only 170 yards, throwing two interceptions, and failing to convert a touchdown, but Adam Vinatieri nailed five field goals to give us a 15–6 win.

Next was the AFC Championship in Indianapolis against you-know-who … the New England Patriots. And again, it looked like we were going to choke in the playoffs. We entered halftime trailing 21–6, seemingly en route to losing to our nemesis for the third postseason in four years.

Lost 24–14 in 2003.

Lost 20–3 in 2004.

And now this.

At halftime, not a soul in the locker room believed we could win the game. This had become all too routine. You make it this far. Then New England tramples your dreams.

In the second half, I was standing on the sideline with kicker Adam Vinatieri, whom we acquired from the Patriots in the offseason, when he looked at me and said, "I hate these (expletives)." We all knew, Adam included, that this was what New England did. They thrived in the postseason. We staggered in the postseason. They were a dynasty. We were a twelve-win team in the regular season. They won the Super Bowl. We won the AFC South.

That's when, after a two-game playoff absence, Peyton and the offense returned stronger than ever. Peyton started the half with a seven-minute drive, and a quarterback sneak for a touchdown, making the score 21–13. After the Pats went three-and-out, Peyton sparked another three-minute drive and passed to Dan Klecko for a touchdown and then converted the two points to make the score 21–21. After back-to-back touchdowns (28–28) and back-to-back field goals (31–31), Stephen Gostkowski made a 28-yard field goal to give New England a 34–31 lead with 3:49 left in the game. (Needless to say, I didn't do much punting in the second half of that game.) With a minute left, Peyton completed the game-winning drive from our own 20 to give us our first lead of the game, 38–34. Marlin Jackson secured the victory when he picked off Tom Brady's pass at the end of regulation. It was the greatest comeback in conference title-game history.

We were Super Bowl–bound. But regardless of what would happen in the Super Bowl, beating the Patriots in the AFC Championship was a major breakthrough for our organization and city.

THE SUPER BOWL

The two weeks leading up to the Super Bowl were unbelievable. It was totally chaotic. The world's spotlight was shining brightly on us. The media. The attention. The feeling of being on the brink of fulfilling a

Photo courtesy of the Indianapolis Colts

dream after all we'd been through as a team. As I said at the start of this chapter, it'd been a long road for us as a team, whether it was the on-field frustrations like the losses to the Patriots and the struggle with our rushing defense, or the off-field turmoil that came from Tony's tragedy. The road to Super Bowl XLI was treacherous. And it was long. From a competitive perspective, it was not our best team; but from a Christian perspective, this team was a best-case scenario.

I remember the message our chaplain Eric Simpson delivered the night before the Super Bowl. The text he preached was from Exodus 13:17–22:

> When Pharaoh let the people go, God did not lead them on the road through the Philistine country, though that was shorter. For God said, "If they face war, they might change their minds and return to Egypt." So God led the people around by the desert road toward the Red Sea. The Israelites went up out of Egypt armed for battle. Moses took the bones of Joseph with him because Joseph

had made the sons of Israel swear an oath. He had said, "God will surely come to your aid, and then you must carry my bones up with you from this place." After leaving Succoth they camped at Etham on the edge of the desert. By day the Lord went ahead of them in a pillar of cloud to guide them on their way and by night in a pillar of fire to give them light, so that they could travel by day or night. Neither the pillar of cloud by day nor the pillar of fire by night left its place in front of the people. (NIV)

The Israelites could've had a direct shot to their destination by the Philistine way, the easiest route. But then God "led the people around by the desert road toward the Red Sea," the longest route. "Sometimes, our God is the Lord of the Longest Route," Eric told us.

It made sense. Our year should have been 2005. Every team in the league would tell you we were the best team that year. And when Pittsburgh beat us in the playoffs, everyone knew the most talented team wasn't going to win the Super Bowl.

But God took us on the longest route because he wasn't concerned with us winning the Super Bowl. He wasn't. God was concerned with the kind of people we would be when we did win. On the longest route, we were transformed and refined. That sanctification wouldn't have taken place on the shortest route. As a result of the journey, many of us who won the Super Bowl were

God was concerned with the kind of people we would be when we did win.

distinctively mature in Christ. The pain. The struggle. The fight. The humility. The persevering. It wasn't easy. But it deepened every believer's walk with Christ.

The problem is that we try to coach God to the shortest route. We complain and say, "God, we've been around this mountain three times. There's a straight shot over there." But when you start trying to coach a sovereign God, nothing good happens. We don't get to decide where the pillar of fire and pillar of cloud turn. God directs our lives.

Eventually, God does get you there, but first, he's going to make sure you're the kind of man or woman he wants you to be. Even though playing in the Super Bowl was a great experience, it was getting there that was a greater experience, because along the road—the longest road—is when you really get to know God. And that's the reward Paul refers to in the book of Philippians: knowing Christ and the power of his resurrection.

After a long, long road, we had finally arrived. And the following evening, we were going to watch the Lord part the waters as we crossed through on dry ground.

I wrote in my journal the night before the Super Bowl:

February 4, 2007

It's Super Bowl Sunday! So glad it's finally here. I've had enough of the hoopla, and best of all there is no more anticipation.

God, I'm reminded this week by various things of all the steps that brought me here. When I think about all of the hours in the front yard with Dad, Reg, John, and whoever else, I'm overwhelmed with emotion. Summer afternoons have turned into Sunday afternoons, but not before Friday nights and Saturdays playing in South Bend. This game has been good to me on so many different levels. You've used it and continue to use it as a vehicle for blessings.

Sometimes I try to downplay its place in my life for fear of putting it too high, but not today. Today I see clearly what football is. It is a gift from You, and it is a great gift and one that has created and enabled many wonderful memories and relationships.

My ability is Your gift, and I thank you for it. I thank you for the voice of my father who always believed there was something different about me athletically. He always said I could do this "for a living." Thank you for his much-needed defining presence through it all.

Maybe there are many more games and years to play, then again maybe not. But, Lord I do know this; whether it was the front yard or Old Settlers Park or Piner Center Street Fieldhouse, or "the barn" and fields at Sherman High School, or those beautiful autumn afternoons at Notre Dame Stadium, or running the stairs in the indoor facility, or the Dome in downtown Indianapolis, or this overcast day in south Florida for the Super Bowl, football has always been something you've used to shape me and place me. Placing me with my wife and my people. Shaping me by the trials and hardships. Placing me in unfamiliar places so I would grow. And shaping the future that holds more of your presence and purposes.

What a privilege to have been created and used by such a wonderful Maker. I don't know what will happen tonight or tomorrow or the next day. But as I reflect on life I see that You've done all things well up till now and I have no reason to believe this won't continue. "Bursts of thanksgiving" (Psalm 28:7) flow out of me for your love, friendship, and plan.

The land is before us. Let us go take hold of it.

It was a battle, and it started out rough with Devin Hester returning the opening kickoff for a touchdown. But we eventually settled down and took control of the game. When I came out to punt with a few minutes left in the game, it finally hit me. We were going to win. It was fourth down, we had a 29–17 lead, and the chances of Chicago coming back were improbable. I went out to punt, and the ball was fair caught at the 8. They had 92 yards to go, trailed by 12, and had only four minutes to do it. I remember thinking, *That's probably the last time I'll punt in this game.*

I began to vaguely comprehend the magnitude of the accomplishment we were about to achieve. After all those losses in Foxborough, all those defensive trials, and all those playoff debacles, here we were, seconds away from entering football's promised land. I remember looking up at the clock. There were eight seconds left and no more Chicago time-outs. It was over.

As the rain came down in Miami that night, so did the confetti. And if I'm honest, so did the tears. We had finally done it. We were world champs. I walked over to my family in the stands, and they lowered my wife, Jen, over the edge of the wall into my arms so she could join me in the celebration at midfield. Mom leaned over the edge of the wall and said, "Hey, Hunter, you're the best punter in the world." I wasn't. I wasn't even on the best team in the world. But we were world champions.

We prayed after every game that season. And after the trophy was presented, we went into the locker room and did the exact same thing. Usually a chaplain would pray, but that night I spoke up and said, "Tony, you pray." So the prayer that was photographed and seen all over the world was actually being led by Tony Dungy, not a priest or chaplain. He coached us through a really stormy year and held us together chemistry-wise. And in the end, if the world was going to give the glory to anybody, it was going to be Coach Dungy, and Coach Dungy was going to give the glory to God. The photograph of our prayer in the locker room captured that.

Then came everything after the Super Bowl. The night we won was only phase one of the ongoing celebration. There was the White House visit on April 22, 2007, when I had an interesting experience standing right behind President Bush when he was speaking. He was very casual; then he turned around, walked right up to me, and said, "Any you boys from Texas?" I was standing next to Justin Snow, who is also from Texas. I said, "Well, as a matter of fact, both of us are." We stood there and talked for a minute. It was just a really casual conversation … with the president of the United States. I had to stop and think, *I've just won a Super Bowl, and I'm from Texas, Justin's from Texas, and the president is from Texas. And the journey we all embarked upon led us to the White House.*

We had the Super Bowl ring ceremony a few months later on June 13, 2007, at the Indiana Roof Ballroom in downtown, and it was a big event. Before they gave us our rings, Coach Dungy had a huge gospel choir come in. They were the ones who carried the rings into the room, singing praise music. It was a great celebration. Coach Dungy and even Mr. Irsay did a good job of making certain that first things were first— that God was glorified and magnified in that celebration, even above the rings themselves.

The Indianapolis Colts Super Bowl ring was customized to represent the team that brought the championship trophy home to Indianapolis.

On one side was the word "Faith," which represents the faith that characterized the 2006 team. On the other side were the words "Our Time," which was the theme going into the championship. Every ring had a red dot, which made up one rivet in the horseshoe on the ring. The one red dot represented one drop of blood—the sacrifice of blood made by players who left it all on the field. But I dare say there were some who realized that were it not for the blood that Jesus Christ shed to change their lives, the ring itself would be worn in vain.

Some of us had mixed emotions at the celebrations that followed the Super Bowl. Part of the letdown was the realization that there were several players at the ring ceremony and at the White House visit who were already set to play for other teams. It's part of the reality of the NFL. Even though we won the championship and even though we were a close bunch of guys, that doesn't stop all the transitioning of players between the organizations. An NFL player's value increases with a Super Bowl win. It's the kind of thing you don't really think about until you experience it. It kind of reminds you that nothing lasts forever and life goes on. But there was another letdown that struck much, much deeper. And for me—no lie—I felt it within an hour of the final whistle.

Not many players reach the pinnacle of success and become Super Bowl champions. The worldwide attention you receive is incredible. And don't get me wrong, I'm very thankful to have had the opportunity to play for a team that went all the way to the Super Bowl and won. It's what kids dream of. But it also reveals a depressing reality for those who lived their entire lives in pursuit of that moment.

Emptiness.

I remember feeling it on the field after the game but fighting it off and just trying to enjoy the victory instead. This was the Super Bowl, after all.

I felt it even more on the plane ride back to Indianapolis. Senior Executive Vice President Pete Ward came over the intercom and said, "Welcome to your first responsibility as world champions. There are tens of thousands of people in Indianapolis right now. It's four degrees back at home. But this is what we're going to do. We'll land, get on buses, put on winter gear, go to the Colts complex, get back on buses, and then get on floats that will take us into a packed-out RCA Dome with all of the screaming fans inside."

All the players and coaches were exhausted. But the realization that we were world champions and had just achieved the ultimate prize in the professional football realm was still fresh in our minds, fueling us with an excitement and eagerness to return home.

I remember looking at Eric on the plane. "So this is it?" I asked. "This is the top of the stack, huh? This is it?"

Emptiness.

The Jersey Effect

This book is about two things. It's about the influence a jersey can have on the athlete who wears it *and* about the impact an athlete can have with his or her jersey. That's the heart of the jersey effect. It's about recognizing the potential harm a jersey can cause—the self-centeredness, greed, immaturity, larger-than-life mentality, and obsession with this world—but also the potential power one's jersey has for the good of society and, most importantly, the good of Christ's kingdom.

I've addressed these issues in the context of the 2006 Super Bowl season, as this year marks the five-year anniversary of that remarkable accomplishment. Ten of my teammates and coaches from that 2006 Colts season have decided to help me on this project—guys like Tony Dungy, Jeff Saturday, Tarik Glenn, and Jim Caldwell. They believed in this project enough to make themselves vulnerable as they transparently address their personal struggles and character flaws that the Super Bowl exposed

> *It's about recognizing the potential harm a jersey can cause—the self-centeredness, greed, immaturity, larger-than-life mentality, and obsession with this world—but also the potential power one's jersey has for the good of society and, most importantly, the good of Christ's Kingdom.*

in their lives. In some of those stories, we learn about the dangers of the jersey. For others, the Super Bowl made their godly influence on this world even more impactful and meaningful.

Athletics are just like the jersey. They can have a positive effect, but they can also be negative. You see, sports have the power to unite us and divide us, to ignite deep passions, to build community, and to amplify the voice of the athletes and coaches. People, like it or not, seem to listen a little more attentively to those who have worn a jersey. We are persuaded by athletes to buy all sorts of things. Athletes have long stumped for products from razors to cars to beer. Sports, fame, and fortune are usually fleeting. Legends are made and forgotten. Championship rings are won, soon becoming distant memories for all but the most loyal fans. Seventy-eight percent of all NFL players are divorced, bankrupt, or unemployed two years after leaving the game. Downright unhappy. We can all point to countless athletes

Photo courtesy of the Indianapolis Colts

who have fallen from grace because of handgun incidents, driving under the influence of drugs and alcohol, domestic violence, public divorce, and child custody battles. We see it every day on ESPN. At some level we are affected by it, and our young athletes and parents are left wondering: is this what it means to be a professional athlete?

In order to address the startling statistics, Coach Dungy, who passionately believes in *The Jersey Effect*, teaches that athletes must grow in four key dimensions: academically, athletically, socially, and spiritually. According to Tony, the jersey effect represents a powerful way to live your life. It is not just about influence, it's about a full 360-degree impact on those around us. It's about sowing and reaping. It's about iron sharpening iron. It's about pursuing the ultimate prize, which has little to do with a ring or a trophy.

Tony says that the NFL is a "laboratory for life" where most people around you have taken sports out of perspective and made it the "end all" of life's focus. Fame and fortune can hijack even the most well-intentioned players, as you'll read in the upcoming chapters. The lies are

subtle—like athletics are what matters most, or you must win at all cost, or fame can bring you happiness. But they're compelling lies that destroy. This book points out many of those lies so you can recognize them and then fight against them before they take your life captive … or even your soul.

This book isn't just for athletes. Everyone, you see, has a jersey—whether you're a CEO of a business or a fourth-grader playing in little league football. Each person has a jersey God wants to use as a platform to bring

Photo courtesy of the Indianapolis Colts

others to him, but the devil, in opposition, hopes to use it as a weapon to turn our hearts toward self.

The crux of the epidemic, I believe, is this: *importance* versus *value*. Athletes in particular are raised to believe they're important. Because of their skills, because of their performance, they are told by family, coaches, and friends that they're important. Importance, however, is performance-based. Importance doesn't last. Importance is empty. Everything that man accomplishes can easily be undone. Peyton Manning, arguably the best quarterback to play the game—cut. Tim Tebow, the best thing that happened to Denver in 2011 as he led the Broncos to the playoffs—traded and forgotten.

As a result, what we're doing as a society is raising people who are very important. But they don't have value. Then, when athletes finish their careers, their importance is stripped away and they don't see themselves as valuable. That's why we have the crisis we do in sports. That's why it's so difficult for athletes to retire. That's why athletes are notoriously in the news after their careers are over; they receive attention—whether good or bad—and that makes them feel important again.

The answer, as I've said, is this: value. But how do you teach value over importance? Understand that you, yourself, are valued. How do you see yourself as valuable? Understand that a price was paid for you. How was a price paid for you? Jesus Christ died on the cross for you. Without Jesus, you'll go through life trying to feel important. And the thing is you can't ever feel important enough. Believe me. After the Super Bowl, many of my teammates and I felt *empty*. We felt important—no doubt. But there's no value in a trophy. There's only value at the cross.

That's the battle we face. And that's the war that was waged the night we won the Super Bowl. Winning the Super Bowl was a great feeling, but if that is all your life is identified with—if the purpose of your jersey is to merely satisfy yourself—then your world becomes awfully small. I promise you that every believer and nonbeliever on that plane flying back to Indianapolis had this thought cross his mind: *There has to be more than this.*

In an interview a few years ago on *60 Minutes*, New England quarterback Tom Brady said exactly this: "Man, I'm making more money now than I thought I could ever make playing football. Why do I have three Super Bowl rings and still think there is something greater out there for me? Maybe a lot of people would say, 'Hey, man, this is what it is. I have reached my goal, my dream, my life'—me I think, God, it's got to be more than this."

You accomplish something that is the number one objective in a lot of people's lives, yet a feeling of incompleteness screams from the winners of the Super Bowl plane. There is loneliness—as if a rodent is eating at your heart. The human heart, from a worldly perspective, is never satisfied.

When you achieve what you thought would satisfy you and it lets you down, there is a window.

A window into the soul.

CHAPTER 2

JEFF SATURDAY

AFTER THE VICTORY: DIVINE APPOINTMENTS AND DEFICIENCIES OF THE HEART

Photo courtesy of the Indianapolis Colts

#63
Center
Height: 6' 2"
Weight: 295
Age: 36
Born: June 18, 1975, Atlanta, Georgia
College: University of North Carolina
Experience: 13 seasons (Colts)
High School: Shamrock High School, Decatur, Georgia

"I firmly believe that any man's finest hour, the greatest fulfillment of all that he holds dear, is that moment when he has worked his heart out in a good cause and lies exhausted on the field of battle—victorious."
                                                            –Vince Lombardi

To Jeff Saturday, Super Bowl champion, Indianapolis Colts, center

Jeff,

I will never forget walking off the field together after we lost to the San Diego Chargers in the playoffs to end the '08 season. It was the last time I would walk off the field wearing a Colts jersey. I think we both knew it would be the end for one or both of us. I'm glad it was my last one. Peyton needed a center, not a punter.

We were both signed in '99, and as I recall, neither of us had any expectations of actually making it. Another team had already cut you, and I was just happy to wear the helmet for a practice and say, "Hey, I did it." Amazing what the right opportunity can afford, isn't it, my brother?

Walking with you for ten years on that team and in this city is one of the great privileges of my adult life. It is nothing short of miraculous to see how God has saved us, changed us, and wiped away the checkers from our checkered pasts. The man you have become and the testimony that flows out of your life are some of the strongest evidences of God's power and love I have seen. Who would've thought that bummed-out kid in a Honda Civic hatchback (egg car) with hippie bumper stickers would become the man you've become?

Over the years I have seen you handle celebrity well. As we have discussed, we both "drank the Kool-Aid" that causes us to "help" God by doing our own thing. It's the subtle deception that God somehow needs us and is privileged to have us on his side. Thankfully, he has been gracious to us. He has shown us both the blessing of sharing in his nature and his purposes. He isn't in heaven saying, "Oh no! What do I do if these Christian professional athletes don't help me?" No, he is fully at the helm of humanity's destiny with no need of our help. How amazing that he chooses us and allows us to be a part!

Over the years I have seen you handle what the world calls "fame" or "status" with grace. I know you haven't been perfect, but you've certainly weathered the storm of celebrity. From the countless autographs you've signed after a hard day at training camp, to the kids you've visited at hospitals away from the cameras, to the hours of service, time, and resources you've donated specifically to plant churches and advance the kingdom of God, I've seen the light and compassion of Christ gleaming through you. Your lifestyle of giving in all realms, without a doubt, proves where your heart is and why you wear the jersey.

You are qualified, my friend. Qualified by the blood of Christ and a life that stands for him.

Sincerely,

Hunter

Jeff Saturday Remembers

"God moments" are circumstances unexplainable outside the realm of God.

During the week before the AFC Championship against the New England Patriots, I talked with my friend Dave Jamerson, who is an outreach pastor and former NBA player. I remember Dave telling me how he had just watched *Miracle*, a movie about the 1980 USA Olympic hockey team.

Before the match against Russia, the head coach of the USA team, Herb Brooks, delivered an inspirational speech to his players. Dave shared the clip with me in preparation for our game against the Patriots. This is what Brooks said:

Great moments … are born from great opportunity. And that's what you have here, tonight, boys. That's what you've earned here tonight. One game. If we played 'em ten times, they might win nine. But not this game. Not tonight. Tonight, we skate with them. Tonight, we stay with them. And we shut them down because we can! Tonight, we are the greatest hockey team in the world. You were born to be hockey players. Every one of you. And you were meant to be here tonight. This is your time. Their time is done. It's over. I'm sick and tired of hearing about what a great hockey team the Soviets have. Screw 'em. This is your time. Now go out there and take it.

Some people may say the USA's victory over the Russians was a "God moment." Isn't that what "miracle" means? Miracle is defined as something not explainable by natural or scientific laws and is therefore considered to be the work of a divine.

In the same way, our comeback victory against the Patriots was a miracle.

Now, I use that term loosely. I'm not saying God wanted us to win that game. I don't know if God cares about the outcome of sporting events. But if anything ever felt like a "God moment" or a "miracle," that 38–34 win against New England did. Why? Because it was improbable. It was unexplainable. It was unlike anything I'd ever felt before.

Photo courtesy of the Indianapolis Colts

As you know, the 2006 season had been an exhausting year for us. It started off well, but we kind of tanked toward the end. As a team, we weren't nearly as successful as we were in 2005. And for the first time in a long time, we weren't the favorite with people in Indiana or across the country. People began to jump off our bandwagon. People began to say that we couldn't stop the run, couldn't run the ball, and were becoming ineffective. In the previous season, we kind of felt like we were a crown of the NFL. Not in 2006.

When we advanced to the AFC Championship, however, we began to believe we could do it. Our run defense showed up, and we really started to mesh as a team. The New England game happened to be one of the biggest games of my career—not just as a team, but also personally.

With 13:24 left in the game, our running back, Dominic Rhodes, fumbled on the 1-yard line, a near-crushing blow to our comeback hopes. But I happened to be in the right place at the right time and recovered the fumble in the end zone for a touchdown, tying the game 28–28. One of the Patriots' offensive linemen scored a touchdown earlier as well, making it the first game in NFL playoff history where two offensive linemen on opposing teams scored a touchdown.

But my role wasn't over in that game.

I ended up providing a key block on Vince Wilfork as our running back, Joseph Addai, ran up the middle for the game-winning touchdown with just over a minute remaining, our first lead in the AFC Championship. People may not realize this, but Wilfork is a 325-pound nose tackle. Let me remind you that I was a 285-pound center. That block shouldn't have happened.

The attention that I received from that game was incredible, and I thanked God for giving me those moments of influence in my athletic experience. Again, I don't know if God wanted us to win that game. But for me, it was a "God moment" because it was the single greatest game for us as a team and for me individually. And the only place I could look was at God.

Down the road, unfortunately, that game also had a negative impact on me. As did the Super Bowl. As did the realization that I was a cornerstone to the Colts franchise. Winning a Super Bowl, for some reason, puts you on a different level. It's not fair to others, because I was not a better player after winning the Super Bowl than I was before I won the Super Bowl. But people cling to the title "Super Bowl champion," when, in reality, I know that all I did was win one more game. The only difference in the Super Bowl is the media attention. That's it. But it doesn't matter; people will continue to put you on a pedestal because you have a Super Bowl ring. And you can either shrug it off, realizing you aren't any different, or you can believe the lie that you truly are something special. When I signed a big contract with the Colts in 2004, I began to believe I was special. I became greedy. Success, you see, reveals deficiencies in your life. There's just something about this world that begs you to serve it.

After our Super Bowl victory, I suddenly realized how far I'd fallen. For the past two years, I'd been serving the world instead of God. When things are going that good, it's so easy to just coast. As a Christian, I understand the importance of building the kingdom for God and doing good things in the community. But when you experience a high level of success, you truly see the motives of your heart.

I found that out the hard way.

After my contract in 2004, I was presented with a plethora of opportunities, and I selfishly tried to take them all. In hindsight, I needed to heed the advice I give my own kids when I tell them, "Don't just do things for the sake of doing them; do things because you feel this is what God has called you to do. Do things God has given you the heart to do."

I didn't do that. I did everything—whether God gave me the heart for it or not.

There's a difference between doing a good deed in the community for the sake of publicity and truly doing an act of kindness out of a desire to "love your neighbor as yourself." If you continually do things for the sake of publicity, then popularity (something of this world) becomes your primary focus and the world consequently hijacks your faith.

I started believing the things other people said about me. People told me that I was an exceptional businessman. People said I was a really smart guy who should enter the business world. Heck, I earned a business degree from the University of North Carolina and had a number of postfootball business ventures. Why shouldn't I?

So instead of remaining focused on the job God had given me as a football player, I became a two-headed monster, trying to be as successful off the field in business as I was on the field in football. There's a word for it. It's called greed. I wanted to be known as a successful businessman in the city of Indianapolis. I wanted to be known as a mover and a shaker. That desire crept inside me. I became obsessed with chasing something else. I bought into the lie that I deserved all the money God had blessed me with. And not just that, but I deserved more. Making more money became the subtle thing that crept into my life and actually revealed a deficiency in my character.

There was a time when I thought, *How great would it be to have a "Saturday Chevrolet" in Indianapolis? How cool is that?* I've learned that jumping at business deals, building a restaurant with your name on it, or buying a car dealership may not be a great idea. This may sound silly, but these are the things that are brought to a professional athlete and laid at his feet.

I had to step back and think, *Wait a minute. I don't know the first thing about cars, and I'm going to own an entire car dealership?* I wish I could've realized at the time what I was an expert on: football. Perhaps I could've focused on my ministry there. But I didn't. The truth in a man's heart is revealed in these kinds of decisions.

After a while, I became so swallowed up in trying to keep up with business deals, it began to run my life. Instead of being focused on how many guys in my locker room I could reach for Christ, I was too busy trying to chase something else. I should have embraced the credibility God had already blessed me with in my football career and used that to impact people's lives and marriages for good. But I wanted to fabricate a whole new credibility in business. It was unnecessary.

During those times of my life, my wife and other close friends would ask me why I was involved in these other things. "Why?" my wife would ask me. "We don't need this."

"Oh, you don't know anything about business," I'd tell her. And I'd ignore her counsel, believing I was on the right track. I can't begin to explain how many hours with my children and family I lost—all because I was chasing things God didn't ever want me to have. But the world did.

We desire to have our name on a restaurant or a car dealership so the world will look at us and think, *Wow, he made it.* They don't know that I'm losing money hand over fist in this business deal. They don't know what a drain it's placed on my life—that I'm not spending time with my kids, that my wife and I are squabbling, that my mind is restless because of all my commitments.

There's something about the world that begs you to serve it.

I can look at my wife today in a spirit of repentance because I know I messed up. I now recognize that, between my contract in 2004 and the Super Bowl, I was dealing with character flaws revealed by success. This "chasing of a dream" for me became success in business. But as I chased it, I became the "double-minded man." I strived for worldly prosperity.

Sadly, this concept has also penetrated the church. The "prosperity gospel" that many Christians hold to in our culture is not a biblical concept. Of course, God blesses people for making right choices, but they aren't necessarily financial blessings. They're spiritual blessings. You don't do it the right way to make a name for yourself. You do it the right way to proclaim God. And that itself is fulfilling because you are pleasing the One who gave you life. There are many people who

There's something about the world that begs you to serve it.

live very foul lifestyles who are wealthy, and there are many admirable Christians who are poor. Your financial status is not God's stamp of approval on your life, nor is your lack of finances. The issues of your heart, the person you are in the core of your character, are far more important than the amount of money in your bank account.

As an athlete, I've also noticed that people in the church tend to cling to the prosperous people in their congregation. It's strange, really. Even those who attend church regularly will place athletes on a high pedestal. There may be many other Christians in a church congregation who are far more godly in character and wisdom, but the church has embraced our American cultural tendencies in lifting up athletes as people who are more special than the rest. The church, like the world, wants to be associated with prosperity.

I'm amazed how many people ask my opinion about things just because I'm an athlete. And usually, I have no knowledge to answer their question. They assume that God has anointed particular athletes with success. But in reality, the average fan doesn't know the personal life of those athletes. They don't know how I live my life or how I treat my family. They really don't know who I am as a Christian. They just know I won a Super Bowl and I'm a Christian, so the assumption is that it's a reflection of God's blessing. Sometimes, I feel there is a real insecurity in the church, and it needs to validate its existence. So the church needs Jeff Saturday on its team. It needs people like Kurt Warner to validate its legitimacy. It's almost as if the church is saying, "If there is a Super Bowl

Photo courtesy of the Indianapolis Colts

champion in our congregation, that gives God more credibility." But God doesn't need us to give him more credibility.

If I were to look at how God has shaped my character—amidst my sinful experiences with prosperity, distractions, and worldly pursuit—I must say that God has taken the mountaintop experiences of this world to reveal my true character and deepest flaws. Those lessons on top of the mountain have routinely lowered me into the valley, where I'm able to reprioritize and return to my foundation in Christ.

Those are the true "God moments" in life.

HUNTER REFLECTS

I was sitting in our kitchen, holding my guitar, when I realized something: I had lost myself. I had lost myself in this world.

I remember hearing Willie Franklin preach when I was seventeen years old. Willie used to play for the Baltimore Colts and then became a renowned minister and excellent preacher. Something struck me that day. Here was a guy who was making a vast impact after his football career was over. He traveled around and influenced young people for

God. That was huge for me. It ignited a desire to give back, a desire to always keep my focus on Christ and make an impact for his kingdom.

But along the way, I was hijacked by fame and status. Like Jeff, I found people flocking to me, saying that I was so important and so talented. I had it all wrong. And before I knew it, I was doing things solely for my own acclaim. I wanted money and a position in the city. I wanted to be a Christian icon. It sounds crazy, but I'm telling you the truth. Becoming a Christian icon like Tony Dungy became a goal for me. And ironically, it wasn't about God. It was about me.

As I was sitting in the kitchen, this phrase came to me: "a time to die." I began to write.

Here I am alone again
The rise and fall against the wind
Alive I'll be the last to carry on
I see the writing on the wall
For every dream to crash and fall
And tremble like the darkness at the dawn

This is the time to die
This is the time to separate
This is the time to celebrate
Leaving this world behind
The time to die
The waters have risen high again
And all of my idols tremble in
The wake of Your love divine

So raise me from my bended knees
Who bow to things that cannot see
And lift me to a place where I stand
Replace my heart and all I lack
And place the wood upon my back
The cross of my dear Lover, Savior, Friend

So take my dreams and take my wealth
And all betrayal You have felt
Take them as a tool for sacrifice
To work to kill or even still
Your Kingdom dreams to fulfill
Today this altar is my stage for life

I wrote this song and recorded it with my old band Connersvine. The phrase comes from Ecclesiastes 3, and something about it made me

Photo courtesy of the Indianapolis Colts

realize that I had made this all about myself. Like Jeff, I too had become greedy and self-centered. God was calling me to recognize my vulnerability to the world, deny it, and then fall flat on my face in worship. He wanted me to "leave the world behind" as "all of my idols tremble in the wake of His love divine." He wanted me to surrender "my dreams and my wealth" and proclaim that his "altar is my stage for life." Not the Super Bowl's altar. Not the Colts' altar. Not my altar. his altar. There's importance in the Super Bowl's altar; but there's true value and fulfillment at God's altar.

It's so easy to focus on our altar, as King Solomon did in the Old Testament. He spent almost twice as much time building his own palace as he did building God's temple. First Kings 6:38–7:1 states, "... the temple was finished in all its details according to its specifications. He had spent seven years building it. It took Solomon thirteen years, however, to complete the construction of his palace" (NIV).

I believe King Solomon is the perfect example for an NFL Christian football player. Jeff and I, after all, even though we were focused on ourselves, were still building God's temple. That's not the issue. The issue is this: which temple were we making the priority?

We were committing the same sin Solomon was guilty of. We were metaphorically devoting twice as much time and energy to building our own temples while God was left with our leftovers. Our chaplain, Eric Simpson, says that living like that is comparable to "tipping God instead of bringing him an offering that's grounded in sacrifice." It's like saying, "Here God, I'll give you 10 percent of the tab."

There are few people who have handled success well. Even in the Bible there are few characters who handled worldly success well. Take David, for example. He slept with Bathsheba—pretty much destroyed his life. And that's why this issue is so important. Success causes the death of so many prosperous people and is spiritually destructive.

There is another valuable lesson about success in Exodus 33. God tells Moses to take his people to the Promised Land (success), but Moses responds, "If your Presence does not go with us, do not send us up from here. How will anyone know that you are pleased with me and with your people unless you go with us? What else will distinguish me and your people from all the other people on the face of the earth?" (Exodus 16:15–16 NIV).

The concept: success without God's presence is not an option. If God isn't with Jeff Saturday as he pursues his business endeavors,

We need to surrender the control to God. He alone makes our names great.

then Jeff shouldn't pursue them. If God isn't with me as I pursue a career in music, then I should run over my guitar with my pickup truck. We don't move unless God moves. That's the key. That's true maturity.

Too often, we strive for success *more* than we yearn for God's presence. Take Genesis 11:1–9, for example, when the people began to construct the Tower of Babel for one purpose: to make a name for themselves. They weren't seeking God. They were seeking their own glory. They wanted to become God.

If you are trying to make your own name great, like longing for a position of influence in the city (like me) or desiring a "Saturday

Chevrolet" dealership (like Jeff), then that's like the Tower of Babel. Trying to look good all the time is a failed enterprise. The idol of looking good just doesn't work. We need to surrender to the control to God. He alone makes our names great. There's freedom in allowing God to do what he wants with our names. We exhaust ourselves trying to run the show—trying to play the role of savior in our lives and everyone else's lives. Just let God be God. He knows what's best anyway, so let him take control of your name.

But it's difficult.

As Jeff said, there's something about this world that begs you to serve it—that begs you to spend twice as much time building your temple instead of God's, that begs you to seek success without God's presence, that begs you to make a name for yourself.

It's time to die to everything this world has to offer.

CHAPTER 3

BEN UTECHT

DEDICATION, DAD, AND A DISTRACTED HEART

Photo courtesy of the Indianapolis Colts

#86
Tight end
Height: 6' 7"
Weight: 245
Age: 30
Born: June 30, 1981, Minneapolis, Minnesota
College: University of Minnesota
Experience: 5 seasons (Colts 4, Bengals 1)
High School: Hastings Senior High School, Hastings, Minnesota

*"The greatest gift I ever had
Came from God; I call him Dad."* –Author unknown.

To Ben Utecht, Super Bowl champion, Indianapolis Colts, tight end

Ben,

I'm not sure why I pocket-dial you so much. For some reason my phone hits you up unintentionally quite a bit. Maybe it's to remind me to pray for you, or maybe it's because God wants us to talk. Or maybe it's because I shouldn't let my kids mess with my phone. It's probably all of those reasons.

Ever since the start of our friendship, I knew you were special. Only a strong man like you could have his body torn in two pieces (internally), lose his standing as a first-round draft choice, keep fighting, and become an NFL standout and Super Bowl champion. I got to have a front row seat for the whole thing.

Being your teammate through the process of your NFL career was such a privilege. I will always cherish the memory of those early days. I specifically remember staying after practice to throw you passes during your recovery period after surgery. I remember thinking, Wow, look at this guy run, catch, bend, adjust, cut, and so on, and he is coming off a major surgery. What will he be like at 100 percent? Yes, those were special times in my memory. You did a great job fighting back to health and helping us win games. Your hard work and determination to develop into the football player God designed you to be are an inspiration to me. However, you did an even better job representing Christ and diligently allowing him to develop your character.

I know you are not perfect. You and I have both lamented long and hard to one another about the challenges of being a man in the NFL. Looking back, it is your openness and vulnerability in the fight that means the most to me. You taught me a lot about the importance of walking in truth and transparency—even when it's ugly. If people are ever going to finish life's race for Christ, it will take truth, transparency, and vulnerability along the way.

You are a great man, my brother. You are great because God has made you great. There are many athletes out there, youth to

professional, waiting to be called to God-given greatness before, during, and after their careers as well. I believe we are his instruments and voice for this calling.

Love you, brother,

Hunter

BEN UTECHT REMEMBERS

It was January 21, 2007, and we were in the postseason AFC Championship against the New England Patriots at home. At the end of the first half, we headed to the locker room, trailing 21–6. We were devastated.

Coach Tony Dungy walked into the locker room and began to proclaim in a very calm yet confident voice exactly how the second half was going to go. It was almost prophetic. Tony told us we would stop them on defense, get the ball back, score, and at the end, would have a chance to win ... and that we *would* win. It happened almost exactly as Tony said, and as I watched it unfold, I wondered if the prophet Isaiah reincarnate had spoken to us in the locker room. That quiet strength Tony portrayed in front of our team set the tone for the next two weeks as we journeyed to the Super Bowl in Miami.

After a memorable celebration, the team settled down and developed a calm yet serious focus on the journey to the Super Bowl. When we arrived in Miami, I remember being in a team meeting preparing our game plan against the Chicago Bears. Initially, our wives were going to be able to stay with us at our hotel. But Peyton Manning stood up in the team meeting and said, "I think we need to rethink having our wives stay with us in our rooms the week leading up to the Super Bowl game. We haven't done that all year, and I'm not sure we should do that now." Looking back, that was a good decision. It was a representation of just how serious this game was to our team and how essential our focus was on the job ahead of us.

After the AFC Championship game, Jim Irsay stood up to the microphone and said, "First we want to give glory to God." As players, we knew the influence of Tony had permeated the team all the way up

to the owner. But the two weeks leading up to the Super Bowl were such a transition from the proclamation of giving glory to God to being completely swept away in the world. When you are a Super Bowl team, it's as if, suddenly, you

Photo courtesy of the Indianapolis Colts

are the focus of the whole world. You begin to process the reality that you are about to play on the world's stage and be watched by nearly a hundred million people.

I realized just how distracted I had become when I ran out of the tunnel onto the field in Miami.

My parents had flown in for the game from my hometown in Minnesota, where my dad has been the pastor of a Methodist church for many years. Their seats were quite a distance from the tunnel. Somehow my dad had managed to work his way through the crowd and find a spot above the tunnel to get my attention as I came running through.

As I ran out of the tunnel, I heard someone shouting with all he had in him, "Ben ... Ben ... son!" I looked back and saw my dad with half of his body hanging over the tunnel, waving and yelling to get my attention. His arm was hanging down, and he had a look of pride on his face as if the culmination of all his years of fatherhood had come to this moment in time. I looked back at my dad and waved my arm and said, "Dad, not now." I turned away and continued to run out onto the field. After running several yards more, it was as if God placed a brick wall in front of me. I stopped and began to think about everything occurring at this very moment in my life.

It was as if in an instant I woke up and realized I had lost all sense of purpose. The playing field had become my field of selfishness. It was as if a quiet voice from God spoke to me and said, "Go back to where you came from. Go back to see your father." The thoughts that began rushing through me were thoughts of where I came from. I thought of all the years of little league practices, all the people who made this possible, all the sacrifices of my parents from my birth until now. This wasn't just about me; it was *our* moment, *our* accomplishment, and *our* opportunity to be victorious.

> *The playing field had become my field of selfishness.*

I looked up and saw my dad walking away, and I began to run back toward the tunnel. "Dad … Dad!" I yelled. But he was working his way through the crowd, back toward his seat. I yelled again, and in a crowd of over fifty-seven thousand people, he heard my voice. My dad turned around and began working his way back to the top of the tunnel. I ran toward the tunnel opening, and he leaned over. I reached up and grabbed his hand and saw tears in his eyes. "Dad," I said, "it started with you. It started with you. I love you, and I want to say thank you." I turned to go back to the field with a completely renewed perspective. I finally realized that this moment was not just about me; it was about things bigger than me. God brought us here. This marked an important turning point in my life.

And now I was ready, really ready. This was our time, and I understood what it was all about.

HUNTER REFLECTS

Distractions occupy your attention. They shake your foundation. And after the occupying and the shaking, they poison your heart. Why? Because the distraction becomes more important than the foundation.

That's what happened in Luke 15 in the familiar Prodigal Son parable. The son neglected his roots and focused on himself instead. His world became "a field of selfishness," where he "squandered his wealth in wild living." He looked his father in the eyes and said, "Dad, not now. This is *my* time." Distractions seized his foundation. In a moment of importance—the Super Bowl—Ben lost sight of value—his faith and his family.

But then the son hit a brick wall. There was a famine, he spent all his money, and he longed to fill his empty stomach with the pods the

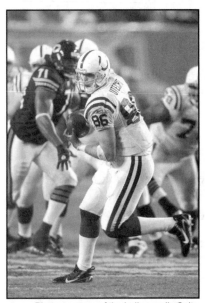

Photo courtesy of the Indianapolis Colts

pigs were eating. That's what distractions do. They're like termites that eat at your house for as long as you let them, until, eventually, your home is in shambles and you're a lost soul. Distractions destroy.

As Ben told his father, "Not now," and began to jog onto that field in Miami, he recognized his distraction ... and he tackled it right then and there. That's the key. In 2 Corinthians 10:5, it says to "take captive every thought to make it obedient to Christ" (NIV). We're fallen people bent to pursue distractions, and we live in a fallen world replete with distractions, so it's essential to do exactly what Ben did. We need to take the distraction captive ... then we need to deal with it.

My father did the exact same thing ... but ironically, he was the Prodigal Son. He neglected God because he wanted to be wealthy. He wanted to chase the world and knew he couldn't pursue the divine too.

One time, my best friend, John Hefton, and I were sitting in my house, talking upstairs. My father was down in the kitchen. John always had a knack for challenging me and sharpening me spiritually. He looked at me and said, "What's keeping you from talking to your dad right now?"

He was right. So I went down and talked to him about Christ. John and I, in fact, talked to him a number of times after that, as did my siblings and my mother. That being said, I certainly don't take the credit for my dad's decision that day as we sat in his truck on the ranch. John had talked to him. My siblings had talked to him. My mother had talked to him and modeled Christ for him. I was merely there when Dad's eyes were opened to the Lord. God gets all the glory.

It was the last day of my Texas visit, and Dad and I were driving through his one-thousand-acre ranch in his truck. He parked the truck near a bluff in between two three-hundred-acre pastures. You could see vastness of his property—the house in the distance surrounded by fields that were checkered with ponds and barns.

"What's keeping you from giving your life to the Lord?" I asked.

I'd asked him that before. All of us had. But this time was different. Dad broke down and started to cry. There was a different grace in that moment.

We had talked for years about pride. He came from the generation

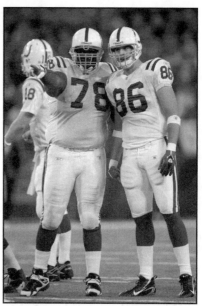
Photo courtesy of the Indianapolis Colts

of those silent, hardworking, pull-yourself-up-by-your-own-bootstraps type of men. I think that was one barrier to his faith. It's hard for people from that generation to admit they need something, because they like to do it on their own. That by itself is an admirable American value, but it's a bankrupt value in the kingdom. It doesn't carry a lot of weight.

After talking for a while, Dad, in his brokenness, said it was time to give his life to the Lord. One of the most special parts of the whole experience was when we walked back into the house and I just said, "Ya'll, Dad has something he wants to tell us." Everybody was watching a game or something on TV. It was a Saturday afternoon. They turned the TV off, and the whole family was sitting there in the living room of our house. Dad spoke up, "I'm going to give my life to the Lord today." We all gathered around him, and there wasn't a dry eye in the house. We went down to the church and prayed together, and Dad was saved and baptized that night—as he abandoned his distractions and admitted his dependency.

Ben caught himself before he turned into the prodigal son. My dad *was* the prodigal son. But they both came back. Ben returned to his foundation; my father began to reconstruct his.

So how do you do it? How do you build your life on the right foundation, especially as an athlete? The New Testament book of Matthew speaks of building your life as if you're constructing a house. The wise man builds his house (or life) upon a rock. The foolish man builds his house (or life) upon the sand. The sands of success and status will eventually blow away, but a lifestyle built on a relationship with God will stand because it's on solid rock.

> *The sands of success and status will eventually blow away, but a lifestyle built on a relationship with God will stand because it's on solid rock.*

Success and status tried to blow me away, too … just like Ben. I eventually realized that my life couldn't be characterized as normal, as I've been given incredible opportunities in the realm of football. I had the privilege to play football on a big stage in high school in Texas and then play for Lou Holtz at Notre Dame in college and then for Tony Dungy in the NFL for the Super Bowl champion Indianapolis Colts. With these opportunities comes status. When you realize you can send a text message to a prominent person in the NFL and get a quick reply, you know you are connected. It got to my head.

There was a time in my life when status meant a lot to me. It doesn't mean as much to me now in the grand scheme of things that I value in my life. Don't get me wrong; I am truly thankful for those blessings that God has allowed me to experience, but my true meaning, the true value of my life, the thing that really matters, is not my NFL jersey, my connection to Notre Dame or the Colts, or any person or position I have experienced. My true value and meaning for life is founded in my personal relationship with God. It's from that foundation that I exist.

This is why I don't have to fit in at the expensive restaurant after the NFL game. It's why I don't have to fall for the temptations of a woman who is chasing a dream to be married to an NFL player. It's why I don't have to buy the most expensive house in Indianapolis or drive the most expensive car. Some day you will hang up your jersey for the last time, and you will have to live with the life you created based on the choices you made along the journey. At that moment, you will be faced with the reality of your life's foundation.

I know much of this book's focus is on sports, but the message here is for all of us who are in any phase of life. Whether or not you've worn a jersey in an athletic sense, I can guarantee that you've worn a figurative jersey at school or in the work place or as a parent. What are you building your house on? Is it being built on the sandy foundation of success, status, and money? Or is it being built on a rock-solid foundation? The earlier you decide, the better your life will be. Be a person who builds his or her life on the rock-solid foundation of a personal relationship with God.

Matthew 7:24–27 states, "Therefore everyone who hears these words of mine and puts them into practice is like a wise man who built his house on the rock. The rain came down, the streams rose, and the winds blew and beat against that house; yet it did not fall, because it had its foundation on the rock. But everyone who hears these words of mine and does not put them into practice is like a foolish man who built his house on sand. The rain came down, the streams rose, and the winds blew and beat against that house, and it fell with a great crash" (NIV).

These truths will always remain a constant in your life and mine: (1) Our life is being built on a foundation, either solid or not. (2) The storms of life will come to all of us. Either we will stand or fall. (3) If we stand, it will be great. If we fall, it will be great. It won't be a bump in the road. It is a great fall. It brings deep pain and destruction, and it is nothing we should take lightly.

Understand the importance of building on the right foundation. God doesn't need my jersey and me. I need God. And despite the devil's fiery darts of distraction sent to set my fortress ablaze, I choose to use my jersey for his purposes and impact people for his kingdom. I don't just need him … I desperately need him. That's my foundation.

CHAPTER 4

DYLAN GANDY

AMBITION AND EXPECTATIONS: DON'T LET YOUR GIFT BECOME YOUR IDOL

Photo courtesy of the Indianapolis Colts

#65
Center
Height: 6' 3"
Weight: 295
Age: 30
Born: March 8, 1982, Harlingen, Texas
College: Texas Tech
Experience: 8 seasons (Colts 3, Broncos 1, Raiders 1, Lions 3)
High School: Pflugerville High School, Pflugerville, Texas

"No life ever grows great until it is focused, dedicated, disciplined."

–Harry Emerson Fosdick

To Dylan Gandy, Super Bowl champion, Indianapolis Colts, center

Dylan,

You are the only guy I played with in twelve years who really identified with my Texas soul. It's amazing how connected we Texans can be. You were born and raised almost a full day's drive across the state, ahem, "the Republic," from where I was born in Sherman ... yet we act like we were raised on adjoining ranches.

One of my favorite Dylan/Hunter traditions is what I call "Country Music Text Trivia." Over the years we've made quite a game of sending texts to each other with incomplete lines from country songs (many mentioning the Lone Star State). Of course, it is the recipient's responsibility to text back with the complete lyric and the name of the singer. I have been all over the country and received these texts from you (and you from me). It may seem like a small thing, but it has been a useful mechanism to stay connected in these years beyond our careers with the Colts. I bet you're the only Detroit Lion who occasionally gets lyrics from George Strait songs sent to your iPhone from a former teammate.

When we played for Indy, we used to text lyrics from different seats on the bus during the drive between the hotel and the stadium. Now we do it from miles apart. It's still fun, although judging from your recent performance (and the time it takes you to respond), I would say you must be searching for lyrics/singers online. That's cheating, and you know it, dude.

There are many other things we share besides Texas and our "techno-redneck" trivia pastime, though. Most importantly, God is the center of our lives. There is no more binding force than God in friendships. Your love for him and commitment to his purposes have always inspired me, bro.

Thanks for displaying obedience and sacrifice. And, thanks for your friendship.

"Amarillo by morning, up from San Antone." Who is it?

Hunter

Dylan Remembers

I'm ashamed to admit it, but my Super Bowl experience wasn't exactly what I had always dreamed of.

I was playing well at the beginning of the season, filling in for an injured teammate. But I had a bad game come midseason, tanked, and couldn't find my way back onto the field. I went from being an asset at the start of the year to feeling like a liability by the time the Super Bowl rolled around. I completely lost my confidence and almost felt like I didn't belong to the team.

Our week in Miami leading up to the Super Bowl should have been more enjoyable. I regret those feelings because I should have been supporting the team; instead, I was small-focused and self-centered. I was swimming in a pool of self-pity. That was a sign of my immaturity.

Life is filled with moments where we find ourselves either playing a bigger role than we expected or playing a smaller role than we envisioned, as in my case. Ambition and expectation can be great sources of fuel that keep us motivated to accomplish great things. But if our ambition and expectations are unfulfilled, we can end up really struggling to find joy

Photo courtesy of the Indianapolis Colts

in it all. That's the message I would share with others about my Super Bowl experience: the lesson of ambition and expectation and the ways both traits can help or hurt us.

Having ambition is essential to succeeding, and with the ambition of giving our best comes the expectation that we will get to play in the big game ... or make a big impact in any endeavor. But one moment, one game in our life, or one experience doesn't define who we are as a person.

Neither does it validate or invalidate us. Life is more than football. It's more than your career. It's more than this world. Unfortunately, I had trouble seeing that.

What if you prepared your whole life to play in the big game and your number was not even called—does it diminish the experience? What if you said something to a teammate on the sideline or in the locker room that changed his life? Which counts the most in an eternal perspective?

> *What if you prepared your whole life to play in the big game and your number is not even called—does it diminish the experience?*

That's the thing. During that 2006 season, and several other times in my life, I allowed football to become an idol. I've been playing since seventh grade and have been hearing people tell me I'm good for years, slowly developing a football-centered identity. That's why it tore me up inside when I was stranded on the sidelines against Chicago. It was an idol.

Life needs to be about an eternal perspective. It's about using your platform—and even using it on a more personal level with the guys in the locker room. I really believe that platform can actually have more of an impact and is critical to the overall mission of Jesus Christ. Jesus worked closely in relationship with twelve disciples. He invested in them. When he left this earth, those disciples radically changed the world they lived in. Truthfully, it's easy to thank God by speaking into a microphone after a victory, but the real kingdom work is speaking truth and investing in others. That's the real jersey effect.

Recently, I was on the phone with Matt Giordano, who played with us on the Colts. (Matt plays for the Oakland Raiders now, and I'm with the Detroit Lions.) I said, "Matt, the older I get, the more I realize what's really important in my life. I have a wonderful wife, and God has blessed me with two great kids, and that's a whole lot more important than football." Don't misunderstand, I do love football, but I try to keep it in perspective. When football ends for me, I have a lot to be thankful for.

That's the heart of it all. Whatever idol you have in life, mine admittedly being football, you must eventually come to the realization that life is much bigger than that. Because when your idol isn't treating you well, it will eat at you and slowly destroy you.

HUNTER REFLECTS

Dylan is right. There is life after football. There's life after whatever you idolize. We just struggle to adopt that perspective when we're consumed by the institutions of man—a product of this world that doesn't fulfill.

Imagine this: I'm a rich, young, unmarried NFL warrior. I'm twenty-three years old, walking out of the stadium to my own private parking lot. There's a cheerleader walking in front of me, continually turning and "making eyes" at me. I'm aware of my own reality. She's checking me out because I was wearing a jersey a few minutes before. But does it matter? The thought crosses my mind, *This girl is very attractive, and she's looking at* me. I'm a Christian, but in the dark places of my heart, that's where my mind went. I could've struck up a conversation, and she would have gotten into the car with me right then and there. That's just one of the many temptations in the world of the NFL. It's that easy. But I wrestle with the temptation and walk away.

So I climb into my high-priced vehicle, on my way to an expensive steakhouse to meet up with the rest of the team, my pocket full of cash, feeling like I'm on top of the world. I arrive at the steakhouse, wearing my cool jeans and rock star boots. Everybody "important" is there. Peyton Manning. Edgerrin James. Marvin Harrison. So are a number of Pacer players. It's not a bad place to be, necessarily. It's a silent auction. There always seemed to be good causes connected. But there are temptations nonetheless. You see, it's a dichotomy. On one hand, we knew we were raising money for a good cause, but there was also a pride knowing that we attracted the wealthiest folks in Indianapolis.

This was the lifestyle of the rich and famous. People are offering me drinks and the finest food. Attractive women are huddled in a group, giggling, and shooting flirtatious looks at me and my teammates. People are saying, "Come over here and sit with us at this booth," or "Listen, Hunter, anything you need, you just give me a call." The manager of the restaurant is giving me his card and telling me to call any time I want a table, and business owners are proposing sponsorship deals. "Hey, I've got a Chevy Tahoe down at the lot for you," says the owner of a car dealership down the road. "Maybe you can do a commercial or something."

Suddenly, I realized something: "I've made it. Here I am at the social epicenter of the whole city. And everybody wants a piece of me. I've made it."

I continued to feed myself more lies, even relating to my faith: "This is where I'm supposed to be because I'm a man of influence for the kingdom of God. And sure, I've done my job by bringing God victory on the field, so now I'm going to take a little something for myself."

Those are the temptations I faced on a regular basis and the thoughts I had to take captive. It's a dangerous place. Perhaps my intentions started off well, but I increasingly became self-centered and drunk with the pleasures of this world, even as a Christian athlete.

This isn't abnormal. Consider Noah. He decided to reward himself after all his hard work for God, so he got drunk (Genesis 9). It's so easy to justify in your mind that you've done a great service for God by bringing him victory on the field and then convince yourself that you deserve an award … even if it's sinful. That's how poisonous and dangerous this world is, especially for an athlete or public figure.

If we take a step back, it is so obvious. Movies, the music industry, athletics, government, education, video games, technology, gambling, pornography, drugs, alcohol, fashion, finances, and the food industry have one thing in common: they exist based upon their ability to make us want more. They didn't evolve that way by chance. The reason you just can't get enough is because you are being manipulated by the institutions of mankind. We all are. I am. Dylan was. There is an unquenchable thirst for more. It was St. Augustine who said, "You have made us for yourself, O Lord, and our hearts are restless until they rest in you." We'll chase importance until we find value.

This world is a strategic, psychological, manipulative force that knows exactly what humanity can't resist. The "god of this world" is at its helm and directs it for its own destruction. Why are we shocked when we read 3:00 a.m. on the clock yet press Continue on the PlayStation controller? Why do we need the latest in jeans, shoes, computers, and cell phones? Why are we swimming in financial debt yet always willing to pull out the plastic for another swipe? Why do so many live in secret guilt and misery, defiling their minds and bodies in the prison of lust and pornography over and over and over again? And why does the elation and euphoria of a Super Bowl championship vanish so quickly? Why does the fulfillment of such an accomplishment, purchased by hundreds of workouts and practices, disappear like a vapor, only to crystallize as a faint memory and a line on a bio?

Jesus, on the other hand, promises to be the food and drink that will always fulfill, as he talks about in John 6:48 when he says, "I am the bread of life." What I'm talking about here is having a deep relationship with Jesus. I'm not talking about doing, doing, doing. I'm not talking about going to church. Not chapel services or Bible studies you only attend because of some crisis you're going through. Not pointing to the sky after a touchdown. And not a postgame interview where you offer some credit to God for your big win. These are fine outward displays, but only if they flow out of a heart sincerely in love with Jesus.

When will we stop playing for this world and the idols of this world? When will we stop trying to modify our behavior or keep our vices in check, thinking that somehow God will be impressed by our efforts? Jesus wants our hearts. He wants our fellowship. He wants our lives. Everything else will follow.

The rich young ruler in Luke 18 went away sad because his heart was firmly in the grip of this world's institutions. In essence he had an unhealthy grip on his culture's version of the "American dream," and Jesus asked him to surrender it. He went away sad, rejecting Christ and the opportunity to follow him. In these modern times, we grasp tightly to wealth, privileged lifestyles, status, and habits, and hold very loosely to Christ. We want more and more of this world and its hunger-creating institutions and less and less of Christ. It is my prayer that the reverse would hold true.

If we continue to merely take a "dose" of Christ, we will be blinded to the life-changing benefits of a deep relationship, lest we forfeit our destiny as the very children we were made to be. The American dream and the message of Christ combine to form dangerous inoculants, immunizing us against ever truly becoming infected with a passion for Christ.

In John 6:32–35, Jesus says to his disciples,

"Very truly I tell you, it is not Moses who has given you the bread from heaven, but it is my Father who gives you the true bread from heaven. For the bread of God is the bread that comes down from heaven and gives life to the world"

"Sir," they said, "always give us this bread."

Then Jesus declared, "I am the bread of life. Whoever comes to me will never go hungry, and whoever believes in me will never be thirsty." (NIV)

This world thrives on creating thirst. Culture, economics, society, government, entertainment, and all the institutions of this world are only able to exist in their current state because of their innate inability to fulfill.

It was during one of the appearances following the Super Bowl that God dropped into my spirit one of the most life-changing truths I have

ever encountered. I, along with a few of my teammates, went with Coach Dungy, Jim Irsay, and Bill Polian to visit the state capitol in downtown Indianapolis. Every member of the state House and Senate, along with every other notable person

Photo courtesy of the Indianapolis Colts

tied to state government, showed up to enjoy the festivities. It was a great experience seeing where government happens. Everyone was congratulating us as we smiled and shook hands with those who do it for a living.

Before long, I started to notice a particular theme running through all of the warmth and cordiality. There was definitely gratitude and excitement over what we had accom-

plished, but there was something else. One politician shook my hand and exclaimed, "Great job, guys! We can't wait for you to do it again next year!" He wasn't alone. During our entire visit at the capitol, we heard a version of this sentiment several times. At first it didn't register, but as the day went on, I began to see past the words to the heart of it all. They were happy that we won. They were excited about what this meant for the city of Indianapolis and the state of Indiana. However, here in

Photo courtesy of the Indianapolis Colts

the days following the victory, when I envisioned pure celebration, there was another reality coming clear. Next year, there was another Super Bowl, and they needed us to win that one too.

It wasn't more than a few days after our Super Bowl victory that I picked up the *Indianapolis Star* and read an astounding headline: "Can Colts Repeat in '07?" These two examples—the state House and headline of the *Star*—made it crystal clear in our minds that nothing was going to satisfy this ravenous need for more.

Now, to some fans, this may seem reasonable, but I remember thinking, *What we just accomplished, what took years to build upon— isn't this what everyone wanted? Surely we can just take a few weeks to enjoy this championship without thinking about the next!* Between that and the forward-thinking politicians, I was taken aback by it all.

Everyone loved the feeling that came with the Super Bowl XLI championship but had already turned the page, looking to the next one.

It was from these worldly responses that I came to this truth:

The institutions of man were not made to fulfill. They were created by man, for man, to achieve his purposes, designed specifically to evoke one response: hunger.

Remember that the world of the athlete is real in a sense, but it is not the real world compared to the eternal perspective God wants us to have. There is the world of the NFL, where players are paid astronomical amounts of money to play a game, women come easy, the guy marries a woman who wants to be an NFL wife, and then his career ends and she's gone. The message of caution I have to you is to anchor yourself in the truth. Don't anchor yourself in a false world, because one day

> *The institutions of man were not made to fulfill. They were created by man, for man, to achieve his purposes, designed specifically to evoke one response: hunger.*

that false world is going to vaporize. And when you are gone, out of the NFL (or any other idol, for that matter), it just vanishes.

On the other side of football, I have seen a lot of players leave it and struggle to find a fulfilling life. But I can tell you this: there is life on the other side when you walk with Christ, when you know who you are and know that he has created you for a purpose and that he loves you.

My wife, Jen, and I laugh about it because life is even better now. It is not better because football was worse. It is better because we are continuing to grow in Christ and in our purpose in Christ. It's not that life is so much better now because playing in the NFL was torture. But it is the next chapter of life, and it's better because I'm with God. I'm growing in his provision. That is where he is and where I want to be.

CHAPTER 5

MATT GIORDANO

A CHAMPION FOR CHRIST OR A CLOSET CHRISTIAN

Photo courtesy of the Indianapolis Colts

#27
Free safety
Height: 5' 11"
Weight: 210
Age: 29
Born: October 16, 1982, Fresno, California
College: University of California, Berkeley
Experience: 7 seasons (Colts 4, Packers 1,
          Saints 1, Raiders 1)
High School: Buchanan High School,
          Clovis, California

"If the light in your life has changed to yellow, I recommend you floor it. It's safer than the alternative." –Jeb Dickerson

To Matt Giordano, Super Bowl champion, Indianapolis Colts, free safety

Matt,

I have a picture from our last game with the Colts. Actually, it was our last play together—my last punt—in the blue and white. We were backed up in our own end zone against the Chargers out in California during the playoffs. It was one of those "just get it off" punting situations. Thanks to your protection, I did get it off.

Throughout our career together, there were lots of situations where you had my back. Your position as "personal protector" explains itself. It was a pretty important one to me. Over the years our friendship has been a place of protection as well. We have walked through a Super Bowl season and a shaky offseason together. We have laughed on a plane flying home from victorious away games over fried chicken and ice cream. We have also prayed for each other and shared family meals during the first few weeks of an NFL season—both of us unemployed. Then our wives have lived together and we both were signed by different teams. It has been, in a word, life.

If there was one word to describe Matt Giordano as a player and a disciple, it would be "coachable." In a generation of prima donna "my way" professional athletes, you have been a great example of the success an athlete can have when he trusts God's leadership and submits to his direction. It has helped to prolong your career. In the kingdom of God within a humanity of prideful "my way" people you are a great example of the fruitfulness Christians can produce when they trust God and submit to his voice. It is perceived as an "old school" trait. Indeed it is. Ancient to be exact. It is a trait the heroes of the Bible possessed, and to me, it makes you a hero. A hero as a Christian, a husband, a father, and a friend.

Life is full of people. It is full of conversations. It is full of interactions. It is not full of faithful friends. I am thankful that you are a faithful friend. Even now as I am retired and you are an Oakland Raider, we stay close. You aren't so self-important that an old retired guy like me is left out of your life. I appreciate you so much, brother. Whether it was protecting me on fourth downs in the Super Bowl or asking me how life was and probing into the personal stuff, our friendship is one God uses to protect me. By the grace of God, we will walk out of this life watching each other's backs along the way.

Hunter

MATT REMEMBERS

Standing out there on the field, warming up for the Super Bowl, I looked up in the stands and saw my wife. It's amazing I even spotted her in all the hoopla and the people. I remember it like it was yesterday. She wasn't jumping up and down trying to get my attention. She wasn't screaming my name. She wasn't telling everyone around her who she was. All she did was give me a simple wave.

Oddly, it felt like we were just looking across an empty room at one another. The interaction was just … simple. And it spoke to me. The message was, "There is your wife; life is still normal; so just relax and be who you are."

It worked for the game. After the Super Bowl victory, however, I was sucked up in the world and realized that life was anything but normal or simple. And like many of the other guys in this book, I messed up. But my Super Bowl struggle was unique in the sense that I used a good principle to justify wrongdoing in my faith.

I decided I wanted to be humble in my response to winning a Super Bowl because that would fit what God desires for us. Knowing that pride was a big trap for most people after a moment of success, I thought about how I might choose a path of humility, which I interpreted as a path of silence. I regret that decision. Now, I realize that "pursuing humility" was a cop-out for not sharing my faith. I was supposedly being humble, but really I was just being silent. As I look back in regret, I realize how much more I could have proclaimed Christ.

We all, however, do this, don't we? Have you ever made a decision to be a quiet Christian instead of a vocal Christian? We justify our silence by saying it's humble or respectful or open-minded or attractive

to others. After all, who likes an overly opinionated Christian, especially when it's an athlete? But wasn't Jesus bold? Like Winston Churchill said, "Courage is what it takes to stand up and speak; courage is also what it takes to sit down and listen." There certainly needs to be a balance in the culture we live in. But we tend to take positive principles to offset the guilt we feel for not sharing the gospel.

I could have spoken at a lot more events—especially small, local events in my hometown. God

Photo courtesy of the Indianapolis Colts

opened several doors that I didn't even see. But I should have. It could have been a way for me to serve God and reflect glory back to him.

My jersey effect could have been so much greater. God desires to use those who make themselves available to him. The problem is that I didn't make myself available. And therefore, I wasn't usable. Maybe instead of saying, "God, use me," with our own intentions already in mind, we might more accurately say, "God, help me to be usable." It's funny how we try to work out our own plans as to how

> *Maybe instead of saying, "God, use me," with our own intentions already in mind, we might more accurately say, "God, help me to be usable."*

and where God might use us. I think we all should be more submissive and surrender to seek his direction in our life instead of trying to formulate our own plan and ask him to stamp his approval on it.

It was a deficiency in my Christian walk as I look back on it now—to call my quietness an act of humility. It sounds spiritual to excuse my silence by calling it humility. But I know in my heart that I should have talked about him more, not just in public speaking engagements, but also in personal conversations with people around me.

I made up my mind from that point on to be the light God has called me to be.

HUNTER REFLECTS

"If I see the whites in that punter's eyes, you better just close up shop."

I heard it. Every. Single. Word. That threat. That challenge. That warning. Directed at *me*, a harmless twenty-two-year-old rookie punter who was last in the NFL in punting average. Directed at *me*, from the mouth of *the* most feared returner the league has ever seen, Deion Sanders, in a television interview a week before we played Dallas at the RCA Dome.

The statement gave me chills all over. I was already nervous whenever I stepped on the field because I was having an atrocious season and always felt like I was one bad punt away from getting cut. And now this. A blatant threat from the most renowned returner in the NFL. I remember thinking, *Do I really belong here?* I grew up a Dallas Cowboys fan, ironically. And here was Deion Sanders calling me out in front of the entire country.

Before the game, Deion slapped me on the butt, as if saying, "Watch out. I'm here." That week in practice, all I did was repeatedly punt the ball out of bounds. That was our game plan. We weren't even going to give him a shot at running it back on us.

When I stepped on the field for my first punt, I picked the spot in the stands where my parents were sitting and just tried to knock it out of bounds.

But I shanked it.

Right down the center of the field.

To Deion Sanders.

The first move he made was … unexplainable. He made the guys on our special teams unit look like they were a bunch of fans whose names were drawn in a contest to see who could tackle Deion Sanders. No one did. And in an instant, he was racing down the field toward me with Darren Woodson and Kevin Williams blocking for him.

A number of thoughts crossed my mind.

All week I've been instructed not to punt the ball to him.

I punted the ball to him.

Now the worst thing is happening.

And I'm about to get cut.

I had a decision to make. In the midst of adversity—when the worst possible scenario was unraveling, when my career was in jeopardy, when I was ticked, thwarted, and overwhelmed—I could either step up and put myself in position to tackle him or I could fulfill his cocky pregame prophecy. It was fight or flight. I could either cower and watch him score or rise up and make the tackle.

I stepped up.

And then—taking into consideration a season's worth of frustration for my punting performance, a week's worth of fear from the words Deion spoke, and a play's worth of outright anger for such a deplorable punt—I pummeled the guy. He saw the whites in my eyes, and then I torched him. Behind that tackle was a culmination of rage, redemption, and a feeling of having nothing left to lose. I hog-tied him like a steer and slammed him to the turf.

I know it hurt him. Initially, he was slow to get up. The rest of the game, he was holding his chest in pain. And in the second half, he was replaced by another returner. I didn't get cut, of course. And that tackle marked a turning point in my rookie season … which led to me staying in Indianapolis for the next decade.

All because I stepped up.

Perhaps it's just a funny story. But parallels can also be made. As Matt says, God uses people who make themselves usable to him. At first, I can't say that I wanted to make that tackle. It was scary. It was uncomfortable. But I put myself in position. In the same way, God doesn't always use the most talented. It's not always the people who have accomplished the most. It's the people who are usable. It's the people who take their responsibility to preach the gospel seriously.

So many times in this day and age, we try not to offend people. In the "name of love," we don't preach the gospel because we don't want to make someone angry. But the truth is this: the world is out there looking for the answer. And it's our responsibility to give it. We weren't made to back down. We were made to step up.

It doesn't mean it's easy, however. Being a Christian in the NFL is difficult. Like the anecdote, there's adversity when you feel like you're alone and there are three Dallas Cowboys rushing toward you.

Galatians 5:19–21, in my opinion, perfectly describes the pernicious state of an NFL locker room and the struggles of high-profile athletes. It says, "The acts of the flesh are obvious: sexual immorality, impurity

Photo courtesy of the Indianapolis Colts

and debauchery; idolatry and witchcraft; hatred, discord, jealousy, fits of rage, selfish ambition, dissensions, factions and envy; drunkenness, orgies, and the like. I warn you, as I did before, that those who live like this will not inherit the kingdom of God" (NIV).

That's the NFL locker room. It's not easy.

I remember a conversation once with a teammate who said, "You can be a Christian and still come out with me. You can come into the locker room and be everything you say you are, go to church, believe in God, but still go out with me for drinks and girls. You can do that. It's not wrong."

This guy talked like a conniving character in an afterschool special on television. He was just that straightforward, blunt, and ignorant about it all. The difficult thing was that I was twenty-one and he a married twenty-seven-year-old. I wanted to fit in. I wanted to make friends. I wanted to feel like I was part of the team. So there was certainly a weight and pain in his words. But he kept telling me, "You can do all

the things that you are doing, all your church work, talking to kids, going to church, and everything—but you can come out with me too and we can totally do this, blah, blah, blah." Right.

That wasn't all. I took a lot of heat for being a virgin before I got married. Guys looked at me in disbelief and treated me like I was a baby. I was looked down upon because I hadn't had sex with a woman. I was looked down upon because I didn't know the things they knew. Now, I certainly wasn't a perfect person, but

Photo courtesy of the Indianapolis Colts

I also wasn't striving to have sexual conquests over women like a lot of guys in the locker room. It wasn't uncommon for a teammate to have some kind of porn or soft porn magazine in his locker, a swimsuit calendar, or something sexual to look at. I made it my intention never to defile myself by looking at that. But it was in the locker right next to me.

Sometimes teammates would try to isolate me. There was one teammate in particular who—even though we were friends—would constantly poke fun at my faith. We spent seven years together—seven years of him trying to get me to fall, magnifying my flaws, accusing me of wrongdoings, and overall trying to shake my faith. He called me "Bible Boy" and "Moral Man," making fun of my values and hoping I'd cave in. He'd tell me, "Hey, you did this or said this or messed up like this. God wouldn't like that." Every day. All the time. And if you're an athlete or even a Christian at a secular workplace or school, you know exactly how it feels.

I won't pretend that being "all the way in" with the guys on the team didn't appeal to me. In popularity, there's importance. But I want to be "all the way in" with God and have a resilient faith and know that I am chasing the ultimate prize—which isn't shaped in the image of a trophy, a ring, or popularity. If I understand that the cross gives value, it gives me strength to resist the temptation of chasing popularity and importance.

I believe God can bless athletes and coaches who are willing to stand up for the Lord, and when they are persecuted for their boldness, it can bring real joy. I think that God's heart is revealed in Matthew 5: 13: "You are the salt of the earth. But if the salt loses its saltiness, how can it be made salty again? It is no longer good for anything, except to be thrown out and trampled underfoot." Athletes and coaches need to train to be salty, so when they do stand up, they are equipped and take seriously their responsibility to positively affect the world around them. But too often athletes and coaches get caught up in the world and try to be part of the world. They can fall prey to its earthly institutions and in so doing are falling short of their potential to shine brightly for God. In a contemporary setting, perhaps athletes and coaches with a proper perspective can be a city on top of a hill that can be seen for miles.

I challenge myself to resist the temptation to blend into the world. I keep reminding myself to take advantage of the chances to affect others positively and, like salt, bring out the best flavor in others by reflecting the glory back to the Lord. I want to make myself usable, even in adversity, and even when it's dark.

The locker room in Indianapolis was undoubtedly dark, but it was also a best-case scenario of the jersey effect, where a group of God-loving players and coaches made an impact for the kingdom. I think a lot of that culture change was because of Tony Dungy. After Tony took over as coach in 2002, our chaplains, Ken Johnson and Eric Simpson, no longer needed to be escorted to the locker room and coaches' offices. No more restrictions. No more strict maintenance. They were on the plane traveling with the team as if they were fellow players. They were allowed free reign in the locker room after practice and games. Eric was on the sidelines tossing me the football as I kicked into the net. Tony understood that the more access he gave to Eric and Ken, the more God was going to use them to change lives.

The reputation of that team was, for the most part, as squeaky clean as it gets in professional sports. People before have asked me if all of the coaches and players were Christians—as if Irsay and Polian simply took a group of choirboys and threw jerseys over their robes. Yes, there are people who have this perception. And I see it as both outlandish and powerful. Outlandish because I know the reality that only a few of those players and coaches follow Christ. Outlandish because I saw the outright hedonism that some of my teammates lived out. But also powerful because of the overwhelming strength of the light of Christ in a few men who, even when outnumbered physically by the darkness, overcame darkness by the power of Christ in them.

There were sixty-three players (including the practice squad) who made up the 2006 Colts Super Bowl team. Those players had an incredible impact for Christ and allowed their jerseys to be used for his glory. But the truth is I was only in deep Christian relationship with a dozen or so of those guys, most of whom are featured in *The Jersey Effect*. That doesn't mean there were only twelve Christians on that team. And this is not to pass judgment on the rest of my teammates. But as Christians, we are either intensely pursuing Christ or we are drifting away from him. And the reality was that the number of Christians intensely pursuing Christ was smaller than you might expect. But the powerful truth is that God can take a small percentage of Indianapolis Colts football players and use the light of their testimony to illuminate a team to impact a community, a state, and even a nation to see Christ in them. A small light in a large dark room will always chase out the darkness to some degree.

It doesn't mean that there won't be tension between you and unbelievers. But one thing that will help ease the tension is always doing your job 100 percent. Players may be frustrated by your lack of willingness to party with them and go down the path they are traveling, but when you take care of them on Sunday afternoon in a big game, they will respect you. The Bible says that whatever your hand does should be done with all your might, so craft your skill for the glory of him who created you. Christianity and a poor work ethic don't go together. If you were a great Christian and you were a Colts football player and you tried to impact your world in the Colts organization but you took shortcuts, what kind of testimony would you have? You wouldn't have much. Christ gave his all for us, so why wouldn't we give our all for Christ and follow him at all costs?

John 8:12 says, "When Jesus spoke again to the people, he said, "I am the light of the world. Whoever *follows* me will never walk in darkness, but will have the light of life" (NIV, emphasis mine).

There are a ton of "Christian" guys who, in moments, want to make an impact and use their jerseys for the sake of the kingdom. But the problem is that they aren't truly *following* after Christ. They're following their friends. They're following the scene. They're following the world.

If you want to be a light, first focus on following. When you're following, that means you are making yourself usable. When you're making yourself usable, that means you're not backing down. You're stepping up.

Though there's adversity, though there's pain, though you may see the whites in their eyes as they draw close and persecute you with hurtful words, stepping up is a concept you won't ever regret.

Chapter 6

CLYDE CHRISTENSEN

Sacred Companionship

Photo courtesy of the Indianapolis Colts

Quarterbacks coach, Indianapolis Colts
Former associate head coach and offensive
  coordinator, Indianapolis Colts
Former wide receivers coach of the Super
  Bowl XLI champion Indianapolis Colts

"True friendship is a plant of slow growth, and must undergo and withstand the shocks of adversity before it is entitled to the appellation."
                                        –George Washington

To Clyde Christensen, Super Bowl champion, Indianapolis Colts, wide receivers coach

Clyde,

We were just taking a walk. A long walk. A seven-hour walk in scorching heat through one of the world's largest cities. On August 6, 2005, we were going to take on the Atlanta Falcons in one of the NFL's "let's extend our borders" games in Tokyo, Japan. But on August 5, 2005, you and I were setting out to be just a couple of American tourists. Normally, the day before a game finds me cooped up somewhere with my feet elevated, trying to recover from a week of practices. This was a very atypical day before a game.

One of the main things that always impressed me about you was your perspective on the things that really matter. People matter to you. Relationships are your most valued treasure. It was evident that day in Tokyo.

When you asked me to go on a walk to see the city, my first thought was, Of course not! I need to rest my legs today so I am explosive and strong tomorrow. *Whether you remember or not, you actually "strong-armed" me into going. Your logic about spending time together and seeing a city we might never go to again ultimately won out. Don't get me wrong; I know football is important to you. I know winning and preparation are foremost in your professional life. However, I also know that your professional life falls far behind your relational life on the priority ladder. So the coach convinced the player to do something "uncharacteristic" (crazy) on the day before a game. Trust me, I have zero regrets.*

We must have walked ten or fifteen miles in the hot Tokyo sun that day. We both sweated through our clothes five times. I made you go to a sushi restaurant with me for lunch, and then we ate at TGI Fridays of all places for dinner. We visited historical monuments and then found, in another part of the world, a shopping district that makes New York City look like a strip mall; we even saw the Emperor's Palace.

But with all the sights we saw, it was the time with you that I cherished most. We talked about God, our wives, our children, the church, your relationship with Billy Graham, and many other things. Such a rich time.

It's a funny thing. I don't remember much about the game the next day, except that my legs were a little heavy, and I think we punted three or four times. Not even sure who won the game, although it probably wasn't us. (This was back during the days when we found it chic to lose all of our preseason games and then win ten to fourteen games during the regular season.)

But I will never forget our walk, brother. What a sweet time of fellowship on the other side of the planet. Thanks for making time for me that day. Beyond that, thanks for always (and I do mean always) modeling what it means to be a man who values people as his greatest earthly treasure.

Thanks again,

Hunter

Clyde Remembers

Together, we buried his parents.

Together, we buried his son.

Together, we were fired and forced to restart.

Together, we won a Super Bowl.

There was no greater pleasure for me than seeing Tony Dungy hoist the Vince Lombardi Trophy that rainy February evening in Miami—not because of the trophy itself, but because he was my best friend. After all he'd been through—his mother and father getting terribly sick and passing away, his beloved son James dying unexpectedly, losing his job at an organization he loved, the playoff losses, the New

England losses, the criticism about his coaching style—he finally accomplished it.

Just remembering that image still makes me choke up. And I'll never forget it: soaking wet Coach Dungy lifting the trophy to the sky. I knew he was thinking about one thing—his son.

My best friend had attained one of his dreams. And *that's* what was fulfilling.

I met Tony twenty years ago at a camp for underprivileged kids in Hilton Head, South Carolina. Ironically, I was helping one of my good friends, Bobby Jones, one of the best defenders in NBA history, with a basketball camp. Tony, of course, was there for football. Bobby and I shared a condo down there for the week of the camp and invited Tony and his wife, Lauren, to come hang out with our families and get to know one another.

Photo courtesy of the Indianapolis Colts

The next day, Tony called me. "Hey, I'm embarrassed to ask you this," he said. "But Lauren was wondering if we could come over again tonight." (Perhaps that's one of the biggest keys to a long-term friendship: do the wives get along?)

"Of course," I said. Turns out, they ended up coming over every night that week, just enjoying a good, fun, pure Christian relationship. Tony and I had a lot of long talks. We realized that we both wanted three things in our careers: (1) prioritize our family, (2) do well at whatever level we were coaching, and (3) use our platform (or jersey) to make an impact.

Our relationship continued to blossom from there. He was an assistant for the Minnesota Vikings, and I was an offensive coordinator at Clemson University, but we still talked on the phone. I was about three to four years ahead of him kids-wise, and having raised three daughters, I gave him plenty of advice. "Here's what's coming," I'd tell him. "Here's how long you'll be in it. Here's what will come out of it." We just went through things together. We enjoyed each other. We'd play tennis, go on long walks (usually before games, when we started coaching together), play Scrabble, chase our kids around the pool, and so on. Our hearts were just knit together under some common things: family, being a good professional, coaching better, and winning.

A couple years later, after the Tampa Bay Buccaneers named Tony their head coach, he called me. "Clyde," he said, "I need you to come down here and be my partner. We're going to try to win a Super Bowl, make an impact on this league, and have an impact on Tampa." I had never really planned on coaching in the NFL, but I prayed about it and decided it'd be a good opportunity. So I went.

In 1996, we started going through the one-year Bible together. We're now on our seventeenth consecutive year doing it, and several other coaches, primarily on the Colts staff, go through it with us as well. Doing that took our friendship to another level. We'd talk about it during breaks at work and apply it to being a coach, husband, and father. We started doing it for a simple reason: to read the same thing—to be on the same page on and off the field. It helped us encourage one another biblically throughout the day and bring about God-centered conversation in the dark NFL world. It united us as brothers—as sacred companions.

> *Lives are perfected in relationship with others.*

We also started going on walks together. Every city before every game was ours to explore. During our walks, we'd wrestle with so much more than that day's game plan. Quality moments happen during large quantities of time spent together. Lives are perfected in relationship with others. Tony was that agent who helped me to perfect my own thinking about the Lord.

We also wrestled with our own roles as fathers and husbands in a field (NFL coaching), which demands so much of our time and energy.

We wanted to help others become better fathers, too, so we teamed up with Family First, a national program that strengthens families and has now impacted millions across the nation. We called it All Pro Dad.

Our constant struggle with our ambitions and our love for the Lord kept us in continual conversation, which led to understanding the ultimate prize and the birth of a program that impacts families. Our jerseys were touching more people than we ever imagined. Relationship is key to influence.

Another aspect of our friendship is something a lot of people don't think about. It's not as big of a deal now because it's pretty common, but at that time, working for an African-American head coach was a fairly new thing. Tony, after all, was the first black head coach to win a Super Bowl. We were able to show that color had nothing to do with sports, with life, or with our faith. We both cared deeply about making our profession better, and that's all that mattered.

I remember playing in Atlanta one week, and we went on our usual walk through the city that Saturday. Tony told me all about African-American history as we toured the Martin Luther King Museum, and it was intriguing to hear his perspective and realize how dear that was to his heart. He told me about his childhood, and I truly began to feel a burden for the things he cared about.

The next several years, leading up to the Super Bowl, were difficult of course. There were the deaths of his parents, the unexpected move to Indianapolis, and the death of his son, James. We were just two guys walking side by side—together. It wasn't about wins and losses. It was always bigger than football. It was about the journey—about the highs and lows.

I'll always remember Tony holding that trophy. But I'll also remember our celebration after the Super Bowl. There was the on-field celebration and the prayer in the locker room, but then Tony and I went back to the hotel before the official Super Bowl party. There, we met with our families and had devotions together. We just talked about the journey and all the moves God had made in our lives. We thanked God for all the rough transition periods that had brought us here. None of us wanted to leave Tampa. Truth be told, my family didn't even want me to leave Clemson when I coached there in the midnineties.

"Here is how God has taken us along," I told my family. "It hasn't been easy. But God has been faithful."

God never changes. His faithfulness doesn't change. And that's consistent whether you are burying a son or hoisting a trophy. God says, "It will be hard here on earth, but I've given you salvation, the Holy Spirit, the Word, family, and friends."

That's what hit me at the Super Bowl: how much I cared about my best friend and how much I loved seeing him excel.

Deep relationships, however, are rare today. It amazes me how many guys stagger through life without any close accountability or Christian brotherhood with other men, and the same goes for women. As a society, we've forgotten the importance of it. The art of friendship has become so diluted. Not having close Christian friends hurts marriages. It hurts your kids. It hurts yourself.

But I'm thankful God placed Tony in my life. I miss walking down the hall at the Colts complex and talking to him about whatever Scripture we read in our one-year Bible study. And I miss walking around all those cities. But God has placed us in different cities for a reason, and now I get texts from Tony about his son Eric's first collegiate catch or first touchdown. It's awesome.

We encourage and confide in one another, albeit from afar … never forgetting all of the things we've done together.

HUNTER REFLECTS

That's what I love about Clyde Christensen. He is one of the most relationally driven men I've ever met. When his daughters were in college, he was the dad who would call and say, "Hey, what are you doing? What, you're studying? Don't study. Go out and have fun." That's just the way Clyde is, to everyone from Tony to his players. He genuinely loves people, and he wants others to experience deep relationships and conversation as well. I'll always remember that walk we had through Tokyo.

As Clyde talked about, we live in a culture that has neglected sacred companionship. We haven't really neglected friendship. Everyone has friends. Work. School. Church. That's not what I'm talking about. I'm referring to sacred companionship—iron sharpening iron, spiritual accountability and refinement, and challenging one another to be more Christ-centered and pure. I'm not talking about simply viewing one another as important. Friends, after all, are important. Sacred companionship is about friendships, marriages, dating relationships, and so forth, where people see value in one another because Christ died for them. There's a higher purpose that goes far beyond importance. There's a spiritual calling.

It would be impossible to encapsulate in a book the entirety of my friendship with John Hefton. John means to me what Tony Dungy means to Clyde. I've known John since I was five years old, and we always thought we would spend the rest of our lives as close friends.

Photo courtesy of the Indianapolis Colts

John and I grew up just down the road from each other. My first memory of John was the day he and his dad stopped by our house. While our dads were talking, we went outside and played on a bunch of hay bales. I was five, and John was six or seven years old.

The next memory I had of John was when he was ten years old. John's dad died on a rainy April afternoon, and my mom took us kids over to visit. John was sitting on the couch in the living room and was in as much pain as you could imagine any ten-year-old boy who had just tragically lost his father. I didn't really talk to him, but as we were getting ready to leave, my mom said to me, "Go over and say good-bye to John."

There sat this ten-year-old boy on the couch with his eyes closed as if he were just trying to survive, and I walked up, hugged him, and whispered, "Bye, John." Then we left. Little did I know then that John and I would forge a friendship that stands today as the greatest friend I have ever known.

We grew so close that we made a pact to spend the rest of our lives together, even if it meant marrying into the same family. To some, this may have sounded absurd, but to two best friends, it made sense. So forgive me for this small journalistic digression, but my journey from self to selflessness was punctuated by some completely ridiculous moments that yearn to be told. We had a pact. We wanted to be brothers-in-law, and we were going to make it happen.

Once, during our college years, I was home in Texas for a summer visit when John and I went to a rodeo together. We were actually *in* the rodeo. Now we weren't riding the bulls. That would, um, hurt. But we decided to enter the "wild cow–milking contest." In case you've never seen this, let me briefly describe this ultrastrange aspect of Texas culture. They hand over a wild cow to you that isn't accustomed to being milked, and three guys are given the task of trying to be the first team to get milk out of their cow. Cruel, I know. But it was educational.

The first thing we noticed was that all the other guys had gloves on. We looked down at our own hands and realized that this was about to get messy. The third guy on our team was my brother. He was in charge of grabbing the cow's tail to "throw it out of kilter." (If you don't know what that means, it's okay because we weren't sure at the time ourselves.) I grabbed the rope that was around the cow's head to hold it steady while John attempted to milk the cow. Since I wasn't wearing gloves, the rope was almost impossible to grip. For that, John, I'm sorry. Kind of.

As the cow yelped and kicked, I yelled at John, "Milk her! Milk her!" (If you're not from Texas, you're probably incredibly appalled right now. But I have no shame.) John looked at me and said, "I'm gonna ride her!" So through all the hysteria, I let go of the rope, and we made idiots of ourselves as John tried to mount the cow.

We earned quite a reputation for our performance that night and ended up attending a dance after the rodeo. It was there that we met twin girls who were farmer's daughters. I know; sounds like a country song, huh?

Well, we decided to date 'em. Remember, we were scouting for wives. If we dated them and put in our time, John and I actually *could* marry into the same family. That was the goal.

As is typically the case, God had his way, and it was better than ours. No, we didn't marry those young ladies. But we did marry girls who were best friends (and we actually loved them and chose them independent of one another). John and I ended up moving to Indianapolis, and we're all sacred companions. We weren't brothers-in-law like we planned, but we were pretty close. Most importantly, the Lord honored the crazy pact we had when we were younger, uniting us as brothers in Christ. And, oh yeah, we're both happy with the women we married. And I suppose we've matured ever so slightly in the mean time. (But you'll have to ask our wives about that.)

Recently John recalls reading in the book of Samuel about the friendship of David and Jonathan. John and I agree that somehow God blessed us with a friendship that looks a lot like the biblical friendship we read about. John talks about being "for" me all throughout life, and I feel that same sense of being for John. When two people are for

> *When two people are for each other, they really do share the heart to see the other experience a full life that is rich in the things that God would measure as riches.*

each other, they share the heart to see each other experience a full life rich in the things that God would measure as riches. There is not a spirit of trying to outdo the other or a spirit of jealousy when the other seems to be succeeding. There is something unique about having a friend who truly is for you all of the time.

John began spending a lot of time at our house. I can't even count the number of nights he slept over at my house on the one-thousand-acre cattle ranch where I grew up in Sherman, Texas. Nor can I count the hours we spent running around in the yard, throwing the football together and jumping off hay bales. We were two boys who just connected. We have the same personality, the same (twisted) sense of humor, and the same passion to serve God and be used by him to the fullest.

We grew up going to church together Sunday mornings, Sunday nights, and Wednesday nights. Don't get me wrong. We weren't necessarily spiritual giants as teenagers, but our friendship kept us away from the vices that ruin a lot of youth in our culture. We goofed off a lot and had lots of laughs, but we were also there to influence each other and remain on the path we felt God had laid out for us.

When John was in tenth grade, he switched from his high school to Sherman High (where I attended) and stopped playing sports. Even though I was a year behind him in school and the starting quarterback, he continued to support me, and our friendship was never affected by any degree of jealousy or competition. I'm as much for John as I am for myself. John is as much for me as he is for himself. We are genuinely excited when the other succeeds.

Now, John is not a football player. If you want to know some of the things that have kept me truly grounded in life, one has been my decision to keep close friendships with "normal people" who live "normal lives" outside the NFL. John is my closest friend. He has had an incredibly deep impact on my life.

As an athlete this has been so valuable because often I have had friends who want to be close to me when I'm struggling in my performance but become distant when I experience success. It may sound odd, but I think it's part of human nature to relate to the struggling moments in a person's life and pull away when success comes because jealousy invades. John has been a faithful friend who has stuck with me through the darkest times of my life, but he's also been there with equal excitement when I have had success. I love to see John win, and he loves to see me win.

John and I started holding each other accountable a long time ago; I think it was one of those things we just stumbled upon by accident. I'm not sure we intentionally decided one day, "Hey, let's be accountability partners!" This wasn't church camp where you ride a spiritual high for as long as you can and call your assigned accountability partner for a couple months. This was genuine, and we didn't want each other to fail. Without accountability in my life, I couldn't have the kind of jersey effect I need to have for God. It's too tough to do on your own.

There are four levels of accountability:

1. Be accountable to God. Consider how sin grieves God's heart.

2. Be accountable to someone above you: your coach, a pastor, a youth pastor, or someone who has a place of authority in your life. I see my pastor on a regular basis and seek his advice and counsel. I place myself under him and give him permission to hold me accountable.

3. Be accountable to someone beside you. This is your peer. The person who is on your level. It's pretty hard to "fake out" your peer. John was and still is that guy in my life.

4. Be accountable to someone beneath you. Establish a friendship with someone who is younger and looks up to you. Allow that friendship to motivate you to not disappoint those who are watching you. If you're in high school, let that be a middle school athlete or a kid at your church. If you're in college, let it be someone in your high school. When temptation comes, think about the generation of people under you who will be deeply hurt if you give in to the world's temptations.

I remember, one time in high school, John and I were on a retreat with our youth group. We were playing cards, and the entire time I was just being an obnoxious teenager, trying to be the center of attention. After all, athletes are used to being the person everyone else is focused on, and it certainly carried over in my off-the-field life that weekend. In every way imaginable, I was acting out and just trying to get all the attention among our friends.

Afterward, John pulled me aside and said, "Man, what were you doing in there? You were really being a jerk." John went on to list my actions in detail by saying, "You did this … then you said this … and then there was this ..." By the time John was finished, I just looked at him and said, "Man, you are right. I really was a jerk."

That wasn't all. Countless times, John also helped me see my propensity to embellish stories. I remember one time John and I were in my bedroom, and he was standing by the window, looking out over the driveway. I had just finished telling him a story where I apparently exaggerated. He looked at me and said, "Hunter, tell it like it is. Quit exaggerating. Quit lying!"

Looking back, those confrontations seem like a small thing, but in reality it was a huge turning point because I realized that early in our friendship, God helped us establish accountability. I'm so glad John had the guts to care enough about me to be honest with me. Because John spoke truth into my life, I've learned a little bit about what it means to be more humble. Without him, I'd probably be a liar and even more of a self-centered jerk.

Photo courtesy of the Indianapolis Colts

You can say just about anything to your friend if you have the right motive and approach him with the right attitude in your heart. And if you do this and your friend abandons you, you didn't really have a true friend after all. John is the type of friend who is honest. Honest enough to "speak the truth in love" as stated in Ephesians 4:15.

Overall, we need to listen to Clyde's advice. The principle of sacred companionship—like Tony and Clyde live out, like John and I have—is fading in our culture, but it's central to our spiritual journeys. In John 15, Jesus said, "You have not chosen me, but I have chosen you. I chose you that you should go and bring forth fruit and that your fruit should remain." That's broken down like this: (1) choose a friend based on your ability to impact that person (I have chosen you), (2) choose a friend with a goal to make them more successful (more fruitful), and (3) choose a friend with the intention to make a lifelong impact (fruit that remains).

There are also three categories of influence within friendships you need to consider. Who am I trying to influence? Who are my influencers? And who am I allowing to influence the character of my life? (This is that key friend who has my permission to hold me accountable—who has permission to speak truth into my life.)

You see, there was an interesting dynamic Jesus had in his friendships. He had relationships with the multitudes and the masses. He fed thousands. He sent out the seventy-two and so on. Then he had his smaller group of close friends, his twelve disciples … and then there were three (Peter, James, and John) … and smaller than that, the one whom Jesus loved, John. Perhaps this was his sacred earthly companion. He still had other friends, but if he'd had to choose one, it would have been John. There's a very biblical backing in Jesus' pattern of relationships. And it proves Clyde's point that we need people in our lives who are close to us. Tony and John encapsulate the values of friendships and influence for both Clyde and me.

That's a main concept of the jersey effect: 360 degrees of influence. One, how does your jersey influence the wearer of the jersey? And two, how can you use your jersey to influence others? But how do you make an influence at church, in your household, in the locker room, or in the workplace without deep fellowship and sacred companionship?

At the end of the day, an abysmal 34-yard punting average in Tokyo was well worth it. And so was a wild cow–milking contest that—I forgot to tell you—nearly ended with a swift hoof to the groin.

It's about memories. It's about friendships. It's about the journey.

CHAPTER 7

TARIK GLENN

FOOTBALL DOES NOT DEFINE ME

Photo courtesy of the Indianapolis Colts

#78
Offensive lineman
Height: 6' 5"
Weight: 332
Age: 35
Born: May 25, 1976, Cleveland, Ohio
College: University of California, Berkeley
Experience: 10 seasons (Colts)
High School: Bishop O'Dowd High School,
Oakland, California

"To be yourself in a world that is constantly trying to make you something else is the greatest accomplishment."

–Ralph Waldo Emerson

To Tarik Glenn, Super Bowl champion, Indianapolis Colts, offensive lineman

Tarik,

I'll never forget something that happened the day you announced your retirement. The story goes that just moments before you took the stage to shock everybody with your new direction, Peyton pulled you aside. He made one last appeal for you to stay with the team. After all, who could blame him? You had been the protector of his blindside over the course of his whole brilliant career. It's very difficult to read defenses and throw the ball from your back. Thankfully, No. 18 didn't have to try very often with you blocking for him. So, it was only natural that he would make a last-ditch effort to save his own butt (literally) by trying to get you back on the field.

He made a very convincing plea about how much he valued you as a teammate and needed you in the trenches with him. But you never flinched. You respectfully told him what God had shown you about life moving forward and then you stepped to the podium to tell everyone else. He may not have been happy, but he was willing to respect your calling and decision.

This story illustrates my favorite aspect of your character. You are a man who is obedient to Christ. When God speaks and we hear him clearly, it is a beautiful thing. When we obey him, there is a divine synergy, excitement, and clarity moving forward.

You were such a model of what it means to obey. No matter the financial cost or social strain, your obedience is a top priority in your life. What touches me so much is the way you obey. It's typically not a blind following, although there are moments of that, I'm sure. Rather, it is a submission, a following out of a deep love for the Father and an understanding that he loves you.

In an age of great misunderstanding with regard to the character and nature of God, I have had the privilege of watching you obey God, not as though he is a rigid schoolmaster, but because he is a loving Father. When we hear his voice clearly and trust in his love, it makes laying down things of worldly importance—like an NFL career—much easier. Thanks for walking that road ahead of me and showing me how to lay down my life—no matter the cost.

Hunter

Tarik Remembers

I could have gone another year. No doubt about it. I probably could have played several more years.

That's what stumped people. My career was still peaking, in a sense. I had just been named to my third Pro Bowl and started all 154 games in my ten-year tenure. Players asked me to reconsider my retirement announcement. Coaches asked me to reconsider. But I had to do it. Perhaps it didn't make sense in the world's eyes to retire when my career was at its apex, with plenty of contract offers and playing opportunities laid at my feet—but I had to discover what else was out there. I had to do what I felt like God was leading me to do … even if it didn't make sense.

I was tired of simply being known as "Tarik the football player." I wanted to understand who I really was in Christ. Yes, I lost some desire for the sport and found our Super Bowl run emotionally draining, but overall, I wanted to discover what else was out there. Football had become my identity, especially after the Super Bowl. I had experienced what the world could supply in all its riches and fame, but I wanted to get away from the world's provision and have all my identity and all my supply come from the one source of Christ Jesus. That's why I retired.

Now, don't get me wrong. I'm so thankful for what the game of football has provided for me. It has shaped me and has helped me provide for my family. The clarity I have about it now, as I have completed my football career, is the realization that my true value comes from God.

The journey, however, hasn't come without difficulty. I was confident with my retirement decision at the time—feeling like I was walking in the will of God—but I don't think I realized all I was sacrificing. Life became extremely difficult. The market crashed, and I lost money. I struggled to find my niche besides football. And if I'm being honest, there were times when I wished I hadn't retired, mostly because of the financial security football provided. Heck, I think I even missed being known as "Tarik the football player." As a Colt, I was at least known as *something*. It's been tough.

But God never allowed me to turn back. And through my strife, I began to discover my true identity, and I've experienced Christ in ways I never had before. It's helped me learn who Jesus is. I've learned to trust God more through adversity, through some financial setbacks, and even through some professional losses— something I'm not accustomed to.

When we lose, Christ becomes the source who meets our needs. God has used those losses in my life to actually build my testimony and strengthen my faith. He begins to reveal his character to you. You can read about the God who delivered the children from Israel, but to experience him is a whole different

Photo courtesy of the Indianapolis Colts

thing. Though it's been excruciating at times, I've understood that Christ is truly sufficient for me. Would I have learned that if I hadn't retired from football? I don't know.

Christ meets our needs in the places where we lose.

Remember that football, or any sport, is a wonderful opportunity, but there are many gifts God gives a person. And the day will come that he will call upon you to exercise and develop those other gifts beyond sports. The reality is this: our society places too much value on professional sports. It is part of our culture. Because our culture puts so much value on professional sports, often it comes with a financial windfall. Just because professional athletes make a lot of money doesn't mean God values athletes more. So don't be confused into thinking that sports are valued by God more than other talents just because our culture puts great emphasis and financial resources into it.

For the longest time, I considered my football talent a gift from God—but perhaps it's only a gift from God because the world validates it. Don't I have other gifts? Of course. But if the world doesn't validate it, we tend to say that it probably isn't a gift from God. The truth is that my football talent is a gift from God, but it has nothing to do with the emphasis culture places on professional sports.

Unlike some other Christian players I know, I don't feel the Super Bowl success hijacked my faith. But it did reveal to me the true values of life. An example of that for me was the realization that immediately after the Super Bowl, I began to ask myself, *What's next?* There had to be something else. I experienced a true lack of fulfillment after the Super Bowl victory that I didn't expect to feel. But through that experience God began to show me some of the greater satisfactions of life that are actually more fulfilling than a Super Bowl.

As I said, at times, my postfootball journey has been difficult. But it's also been fulfilling—far more fulfilling than hoisting that Vince

Lombardi Trophy. I've since gone on mission trips and have been able to really focus on my family. Seeing God work in people's lives on the mission field has proven to be far more impacting and life-changing than succeeding on the football field, even winning a Super Bowl.

Photo courtesy of the Indianapolis Colts

As a parent now, I desire to rear my children with a focus on God. They may become truly gifted athletes ... or they may not. But what is more important to me is to help them understand how God can be at the center of their lives. My kids will play sports, but sports will not be the ultimate focus. We take time to pray and study the Bible together in our family. These things are more important than sports. We have already begun to teach our kids that even in our conversation at home, sports are not the center of it all. Our friendships with others, our relationship with God, and even our family vacations are more important than the kids' commitment to sports.

I'm concerned about parents who put their kids so deeply into sports that it requires excessive weekend travel, demands large commitments of time, and takes away real family life. I just want to tell them, "It's not *that* important." I made my living in sports and have a Super Bowl ring, but that's not what defines me. Football isn't supposed to be the thing you "sell your soul to."

> *I made my living in sports and have a Super Bowl ring, but that's not what defines me. Football isn't supposed to be the thing you "sell your soul to."*

It's really important to understand that athletics are not the ultimate destination of your life. It is a part of your life, but there will be so much more living beyond sports. Coaches and parents need to emphasize to players that the aspects of character building are the important pieces to take away from sports. I love this quote from John Wooden: "Sports don't build your character. Sports expose your character." The learned traits of teamwork, discipline, and dedication are great assets. If a player comes out of sports with a completely balanced life … that is truly the measure of success.

Walking away from athletics wasn't the end for me. To the contrary, it was the beginning of experiencing Christ in a fresh and new way that I'd never experienced before. In the end, isn't that what is most important anyway? Knowing Christ?

I stand by my decision.

HUNTER REFLECTS

The NFL is composed of a lot of players who never really grow up.

Some athletes never learned Tarik's lesson—that sports do not define them. It's made up of players who started playing football at eight years old and have been superstars ever since. More often than not, they've been coddled. They were never forced to learn any real responsibility because they've always had things given to them. They still have toys, but now the toys have motors. They still play video games. They play golf and never have to pay. They walk into a restaurant and expect to get a table immediately. And they marry the most beautiful women in the world whose affection they didn't have to strive to earn. And now they're playing in the NFL at the age of twenty-three and—guess what—they're still eight years old.

That's why 78 percent of NFL players are divorced, bankrupt, or unemployed after their careers are over, as Tony mentioned in the Foreword. That's why NFL players are six times more likely to commit suicide. Sure, they know how to work hard when it comes to football; but their growth is stunted in other areas of development: social, academic, and spiritual. They're not ready to raise a family or provide for their household when everything else has been given to them because they were football players. They're not ready to work … for anything. That's why there is disaster in so many players' postfootball lives.

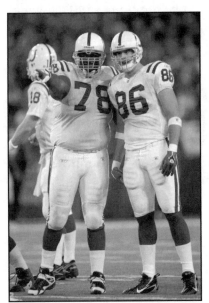

Photo courtesy of the Indianapolis Colts

That's why I admire Tarik so much. He was disturbed with his identity—that everyone saw him as "Tarik the football player." He understood that there was more to life. There was more to his being than football. So he listened to God and—

even though there were millions of more dollars out there for him to make—he began to delve into his faith like never before.

But Tarik also alluded to the struggle of life after football. He missed the money. He missed the security. He missed the feeling of importance. And there were times he wanted to renege on his decision. In that struggle, however, he discovered value in Christ. In his losses, in his dependency, in the things that didn't work out for him in his postfootball life, he began to know Christ at a deeper level—which is what we were born to do anyway. Tarik got it. Perhaps Os Guinness said it best, "We are not primarily called to do something or go somewhere; we are called to Someone. We are not called first to special work but to God. The key to answering the call is to be devoted to no one and to nothing above God himself." That's maturity. Perhaps Tarik realized how young and immature he was throughout his postcareer struggle (I know I certainly did), but he answered God's call and was stronger in his faith for it.

Most athletes think of themselves as kings. They're on top of the world. In 2 Chronicles 26, sixteen-year-old Uzziah was named king of Judah. He built towers throughout Jerusalem (verse 9), he had an army of soldiers (verse 11), and his fame spread to the border of Egypt (verse 8). The young king was the real deal. He was popular. He was talented. He was revered by his people.

Then comes verse 16: "But after Uzziah became powerful, his pride led to his downfall" (NIV). Uzziah's downfall came when he entered the temple to burn incense to the Lord, a task strictly reserved for the priests. Azariah, the chief priest, warned him that he was acting outside of his role. Verses 19–20 state, "Uzziah, who had a censer in his hand ready to burn incense, became angry. While he was raging at the priests in their presence before the incense altar in the Lord's temple, leprosy broke out on his forehead. When Azariah the chief priest and all the other priests looked at him, they saw that he had leprosy on his forehead, so they hurried him out. Indeed, he himself was eager to leave, because the Lord had afflicted him" (NIV).

Like many athletes, Uzziah was a child. But because everything went well for him, because he was given anything, he became his own god. And he believed that everything should be given to him, even the spiritual duties of the high priest. And, as we saw, when he was truly tested with what he could not have, he became angry, God struck him, and he was a leper for the rest of his days. His pride and immaturity destroyed him—just like it attempts to destroy 78 percent of players in their post-NFL lives.

Chapter 8

JIM CALDWELL

The Power of Prayer and the Protection of God

Photo courtesy of the Indianapolis Colts

Quarterbacks coach, Baltimore Ravens
Former NFL head coach, Indianapolis Colts
Former quarterbacks coach of the Super
  Bowl XLI champion Indianapolis Colts

"The greatest tragedy of life is not unanswered prayer, but unoffered prayer."
                                                          –F. B. Meyer

To Jim Caldwell, Super Bowl champion, Indianapolis Colts, quarterbacks coach

Jim,

I imagine being the quarterbacks coach for the Colts was a fairly rewarding position. Rewarding? Yes. Easy to get? No. Easy to hold on to? Even harder. Before you were hired by the Colts to coach QBs, there was a revolving door of guys who, for whatever reason, came and went. Promoted. Hired elsewhere. Fired by the Colts. There were multiple reasons. That job was slippery for a number of years. I find it to be no accident that your hiring brought a level of stability and consistency to that staff position we hadn't had before.

Most people don't realize that for about nine of my ten years, I was the third-string quarterback for the Colts. In fact, only you, I, and probably a handful of others were aware of this. I'm sure that is because no one in the Colts organization wanted opposing teams to know that our emergency QB was a punter who hadn't played the position since college. That might have raised the bounty on Peyton. Or maybe not.

At any rate, you were responsible ever so often for making sure I had a sliver of the offense down. As a coach, I might have been on edge about the unsoundness of our organizational philosophy toward the third-string quarterback position. After all, I don't think there's another NFL team that only carries two quarterbacks. The game is just too violent. So you were responsible for trying to "develop" a guy who wore soccer shoes on Sundays. Safe to say if Peyton and Jim Sorgi had gone down, we probably wouldn't have had one of those "out of nowhere, Kurt Warner, bag boy to MVP" stories with our punter at the helm. Still, as I fumbled (literally at times) through my small learning process, you remained interested, optimistic, and diligent.

Yes, I might have been on edge. But you weren't ... about anything ... ever. Jim, in all of our years together, and even the 2011 season as you tried to navigate an injury-plagued team through a rough year as the head coach of the Indianapolis Colts, I have always found both of your feet solidly on the ground. It is no mystery as to why. That is why I am writing this letter.

You are a man who knows the Lord. I don't mean that just because you have prayed a prayer for salvation, or that you have been through a process of confirmation according to the government of a particular church, or even that you read your Bible every day. No, you abide in the Lord. You treasure him and enjoy him. It is clear to me as you walk through this life that you are in constant communication with God. Yes, I know you have your times of allotted prayer and Bible study. And yes, I know you aren't always perfectly stable in your emotions. No one is. However, as you walk life's road—with all of its undulations—it is clear that you are walking it with Jesus. Isaiah 26:3 says, "You will keep in perfect peace those whose minds are steadfast, because they trust in you" (NIV). When I think of you, I think of a man who is steadfast. A man who trusts in the Lord because he knows the Lord and has tasted of his goodness. What a privilege to learn from your example as a godly man who remains close to God in the storms and the stillness.

Honestly,

Hunter

JIM REMEMBERS

I should have died.

I stood there in the shallow end, watching kid after kid go down a relatively small slide (probably ten to twelve feet high) as one of the pool employees caught them at the bottom. I was an adventurous kid, five years old at the time, and decided that I, too, wanted to go down the slide.

As I sat at the top, however, I realized that the woman at the bottom of the slide catching each child wasn't an employee at all. It was a mother who was simply helping her children. She saw me, realized I wasn't part of her group, and walked away.

I slid down anyway.

My sister, who was six, and my brother, who was four, were at the pool as well. None of us could swim, but we convinced Mom to let us go because we promised to stay in the shallow end. Mom wasn't allowed to enter the pool area because, growing up in a very fundamental religious background, she was wearing a dress instead of a bathing suit. Now, the slide was technically in the shallow end, but it was located right where the pool floor started to slant downward and get deeper.

My body struck the surface of the water. Then it sank, the momentum from the slide pushing me deeper—five feet, six feet, seven feet, eight feet, fifteen feet—until I was holding my breath, sitting at the bottom of the deep end.

There were plenty of lifeguards at the pool, but they were listening for screams and looking for flailing arms. They weren't looking at the bottom. Plus, isn't it assumed that just about everyone at the pool, especially in the deep end, can swim?

All I could do was hold my breath—simply prolong death—unless someone saw me.

No one, of course, saw me. But I saw someone.

Down in the deep end, there were two diving boards, a high dive and a low dive. As I sat at the bottom, I could see bodies plunging into the water above me and pairs of legs sinking toward the floor of the pool.

I didn't have much air left and started to gag. That's when a young man jumped off the high dive. Not knowing someone was beneath him, his feet touched the floor literally right in between my legs. As he kicked off the bottom of the pool toward the surface, I reached out my hands and grabbed his trunks, practically pulling them down.

I think the boy originally thought there was someone just horsing around with him, but he must have looked down and seen the desperation and terror on my face, because the next thing I knew, he was holding me up for air, swimming on his back with me resting on his chest, as I coughed and gagged uncontrollably.

He was probably seventeen or eighteen and had blonde hair. That's all I remember about him. He rested me on the side of the pool and made sure I was okay. Still in shock, I thanked him and then went off to find Mom.

"Go find that kid, go find that kid," Mom said after I told her the story. She wanted to meet him and thank him herself.

I looked *everywhere* for him. But it was as if he disappeared … or as if he had been the one hiding on the floor of the deep end. It was almost as if he were an angel—the way he landed right in between my legs in a desperate moment of need, rescued me, and then disappeared.

On the way home, Mom and I were still shaken up from the experience, so I sat in the front seat so we could talk.

"Mom, I almost died today," I told her.

"I know," she said. "But the Lord protects you. I've been praying for you."

In that moment, even though I was only five years old, it clicked. You see, my bedroom was right above my mother and father's room, and I could hear everything she said through the radiator. Every night, I heard Mom calling out my name, my brother's name, my sister's name, and my grand-mother's name in prayer. I realized that prayer and protection are connected.

What amazed me was that I not only heard Mom pray but

Photo courtesy of the Indianapolis Colts

also witnessed her prayers get answered. I started to pray for myself at a young age; I sincerely believed in the power of prayer. While I was growing up in church, Mom would tell me that when we sang "Jesus is

Mine," I'd get mad at the other kids because Jesus was *mine* … not theirs. I was young, but I believed in an intimate relationship with God. That can be attributed to my mother helping me grasp the power of prayer.

Prayer is something that most people don't believe in. Even most Christians don't live like they believe it, evidenced by their lacking prayer lives. But I have a real, true, fundamental belief that prayer is the lifeline of our spiritual lives. When I lift my prayers to the Father, I know that in some sort of time, the Lord will answer them. I believe in prayer wholeheartedly, and that's why I have a dedicated prayer life. I just think that having a consistent dedicated time of prayer, when you are on your knees in solitude to connect with God, is the most important thing you can do on a daily basis. It's essential.

> *Prayer is the lifeline of our spiritual lives.*

When I think about the Super Bowl, in fact, it's prayer that stands out to me the most.

My personal journey to the Super Bowl began in 2000, right after I'd been fired from Wake Forest. I had three years left on my contract, so I was just planning to take a year off to rejuvenate my mind, travel to different programs, learn from other NCAA coaches, and hope I'd get an opportunity to be a head coach again. That's when Tony Dungy entered the picture.

Tony and I knew each other because he had been a quarterback at Minnesota and I was a starting defensive back at Iowa. We played one another every year in the Big Ten. We were never, however, very close. We just knew one another.

I gave Tony a call in 2000, hoping to get one of my assistants at Wake Forest a job at Tampa. I was at the Atlanta Marriot finishing up my duties at an American Football Coaches Association Convention, and I was just staring out the window, talking to Tony.

"So what are you going to do next year?" Tony asked me.

I didn't know yet. I was just trying to help the Wake Forest staff that was fired with me find jobs, and all I could honestly think about was an upcoming trip with my wife to the Bahamas. I sort of wanted to escape for a while.

"I'm just trying to get my staff placed," I told him.

"Well, have you ever thought about coaching in the NFL?"

"I haven't," I replied. "I'd consider it as long as it's not the same position that I'm calling you about for my assistant."

"No, it's something else. We need a quarterbacks coach."

"All right," I said. "I'll think about it."

Turns out, I ended up going to Tampa for a year. I got close to Tony, and it was tough to see him wrestle with the criticism he was taking from the media and pundits in the area.

"He doesn't scream and yell enough," they'd say.

"He's not passionate enough."

"His coaching style will never bring Tampa a Super Bowl."

He and his staff were fired from Tampa, and it was even more frustrating when the Buccaneers went on to win a Super Bowl the year after. "We were right," the media said. "We had to get rid of Dungy."

I prayed for Tony a lot during that period—that the Lord would elevate Tony for his own glory and that God would do something remarkable through Tony.

That prayer was answered numerous times over the next seven years, but perhaps most notably in our Super Bowl victory, when we brought the Vince Lombardi Trophy to the city of Indianapolis and gave God all the glory. It was as if God elevated Tony for all he'd been through, just like I prayed. And Tony gave glory back to God. It was a beautiful thing.

One of my favorite verses is Micah 7:7: "But as for me, I watch in hope for the Lord, I wait for God my Savior; my God will hear me" (NIV).

God heard my mother's prayers for my protection, and God heard my prayers for Tony, along with hundreds of other answered prayers in my lifetime. That's why I continue to look to the Lord. He truly cares. And he truly hears.

Hunter Reflects

I got quite a few questions from my teammates during my last season with the Colts. Maybe it was because I'd go to my morning special teams meetings and then disappear for four hours before practice in the afternoon. Or maybe it was because I routinely pulled into a parking lot filled with pricey sports cars and tricked-out SUVs at the Colts complex in my dirty Ford pickup truck ... with a canoe in the truck bed.

Yep, a canoe.

You see, in my ten seasons with the Colts, I spent a lot of time at Eagle Creek Park. It's one of the largest parks in Indiana and right across the street from the complex. Early in my career, I'd finish my meetings in the morning and walk to Eagle Creek to spend time with God. I went on prayer walks, kept a personal prayer journal, and just enjoyed being in the middle of God's creation with no distractions. By the end of my career, I started loading a canoe into my truck bed every morning and canoeing after my morning meetings.

I'd bring my Bible and phone in a plastic bag, take my fishing rod and tackle box, and just explore the coves and streams at Eagle Creek. I'd pray, read the Word, and fish (although I never caught a darn thing out there ... maybe it was because I didn't have a fishing license and was technically poaching). I remember walking into the locker room several times just thinking, *No one has any idea where I've been.*

I remember, on one of my prayerful canoe trips, I had a powerful tailwind. I was flying down the reservoir, the wind directly behind me, making my canoe go faster than ever before. Needless to say, I was loving life. After a while, however, I remember feeling as if I were in a different world. There weren't any people. I had no idea where civilization was. And there were even creatures I didn't recognize—huge birds sailing above me, making me feel as if I had voyaged into Narnia or something.

I looked at the time on my phone. It was eleven o'clock. Then I looked behind me. I couldn't even see where I needed to be, because I had probably gone a mile. I had less than an hour to get back to practice. The wind was in my face. And I was the Colts' age-old punter stranded in the middle of a Hoosier reservoir, flirting with being late for practice. But I had to try.

As I made my way back toward my destination, the headwind was so strong that when I stopped to take a break, I could feel the nose of my canoe start to turn the opposite direction. Somehow, I made it back in time and staggered into the locker room, drenched in sweat and overcome by exhaustion.

Justin Snow looked at me. "Where've you been?" he said.

"My canoe," I panted.

Another teammate looked at me and said, "Man, what the hell?"

Justin just shook his head, as if he wasn't at all surprised.

Looking back at my time with the Colts, it's those prayerful walks and canoe rides at Eagle Creek that I really miss—both the tailwinds and the headwinds. That was my treasured time with God. It was when I cried out to him and laid down my burdens. As I look through my prayer notebook today, there is page after page of heavy requests as I transparently opened my soul to the One who cares most about my soul. Transcribed on those pages is a relationship with God that was very alive—even amid pain and confusion.

I remember a few years prior wrestling with a headwind of pain and confusion at Notre Dame as I struggled with depression. I think a lot of it had to do with homesickness—being a Texas kid stuck in the cold northern Indiana winters, feeling, at times, like I didn't belong there socially. When I entered the NFL, it wasn't homesickness anymore, but I think it was a number of issues that contributed to my depression: the decisions I had to make, perhaps my dating life, and a variety of other struggles associated with being a professional athlete. Ultimately, I believe the underlying and infiltrating phrase behind my depression was this: *It's all up to me.*

There were a lot of triumphs and times of prayer over there at Eagle Creek. It taught me about God, and it taught me about myself. That's what prayer does. Strangely, as you verbally unveil your problems to

God, you learn more about yourself. You become more self-aware. And it touches the heart of God when we're honest with him about our issues in life.

But here's the thing about prayer: it's important to be persistent, but it's not about simply checking something off your to-do list. The purpose of prayer isn't about getting things done; it's about *knowing* the Lord. It's about being alive. It's relational time. And that's why I found a time and a creative place to be with God on a daily basis—because above everything, I wanted to know Christ more.

I also had a prayer routine on game weekends. We'd have a Bible study on Friday after practice and chapel on Saturday evenings. On Sunday mornings, I'd get up early and find a stairwell or conference

Photo courtesy of the Indianapolis Colts

room to spend time with God. Focusing on the eternal helped counter my game day anxiety, because most of the time I'd been thinking about the world too much. Before every game in 2006, we'd throw everyone's jersey number into a hat, pick one out, and then pray for that person after Bible study on Friday night. We wanted to live for God, and we wanted our journey to be all about God.

When we got to the stadium on game day, Justin Snow and I would pray together in the locker room. We prayed for all kinds of stuff: our families, the game, safety during the game, and that God would be glorified in our performance. Whenever Justin and I were finished, a larger group of guys would say a big group prayer. By that time, it was merely minutes before we ran onto the field, and we'd all gather around Tony, kneel, and say the Lord's Prayer with a priest. Every once in a while, if the priest wasn't there, one of the players would lead prayer—

but never Tony. Tarik would typically lead it, I think Jeff did it a couple times, and I remember leading prayer once. Right before the game, sitting on the bench, I would pray with Dallas Clark, Ben Utecht, and Bryan Fletcher.

By this point, my mind was usually in a proper perspective, and football was in its place. Looking back, I don't really miss playing the game—but I miss the Friday afternoon Bible studies, prayers in the locker room, and reflection time in a conference room on game day mornings. That's what I miss.

One of my favorite places to spend time with God was at training camp. Even though it was an emotional time—because you had to leave your family and prepare for a new season—there was just so much alone time and ample opportunity to focus on God with no distractions. I had plenty of time to sit in my dorm room at Rose-Hulman in Terre Haute, Indiana, and just … think. I'd always bring two personal items: my Bible and my guitar. So during training camp in 2003, I wrote "Lay Down" for Connersvine. It's a song about prayer—about the importance of routinely laying our burdens at the foot of the cross and treasuring our communication with God.

Listen to my humble cry
Listen to my earnest plea
Hear my voice as I am calling out
I'm on my knees again
I don't wanna go away
From this holy, holy place
I guess I am saying
Lord, I lay it all down again

All of my life I'm
Happy to lay down
In light of your glory
The light of your glory

When I wake up in the night
And I feel you in my room
Something in your voice is drawing me
To follow after you
To the place where I belong
Far away from incomplete
Where I give it all to you
Because you gave all for me

In the morning when I rise to
Lord I lay down
In the evening under skies from you
Lord I lay it down
Every day and all my life from you
Lord I lay it down

The line "When I wake up in the night and I feel you in my room" is kind of a strange one. But it takes me back to a time in my life when I would constantly wake up in the middle of the night and feel beckoned to approach God's throne and lay my problems down. So I'd leave my wife Jen, go downstairs, get on my knees, and just spend time with the Lord. I remember—when my depression was at its peak—getting on my knees and being absolutely speechless. I didn't even know what to tell God, because I was so overwhelmed, but I still wanted him to know that I was willing to sacrifice my time because he was worth it ... even if I didn't know what to say. I was there just to be with God. And I wanted the Lord to know he was important to me.

I want people to know that it's okay to cry out to God. God wants us to cry out to him in anguish, in utter dependence on him alone. That's what Job did. That's what Jesus did in Luke 22 when his sweat became "like drops of blood" as he prayed, "Father, if you are willing, remove this cup from me." Prayer wasn't just out of habit for them. They needed it. It was intimate. And just like Jim Caldwell, I need prayer, too.

I'd even argue that the real jersey effect is impossible without prayer. The jersey effect will be about you if it's not about God. If you're not connected to God (through prayer), you *cannot* truly go and do things for him. God uses people who know him. For me, I know that as God-centered as my actions may be—whether it's playing a concert or delivering a message—they will be

> *God uses people that know Him.*

about me if I don't pray and commit them to the Lord. There have been times when I've preached and have been tempted afterward to pat myself on the back. That's when the strength of your jersey effect is weakened. That's when your ministry becomes more about you and less about God. Inherently sinful people will always seek their own desires and do things for themselves … unless they stay connected to God.

Consider John 15:1–11:

I am the true vine, and my Father is the gardener. He cuts off every branch in me that bears no fruit, while every branch that does bear fruit he prunes so that it will be even more fruitful. You are already clean because of the word I have spoken to you. Remain in me, as I also remain in you. No branch can bear fruit by itself; it must remain in the vine. Neither can you bear fruit unless you remain in me. I am the vine; you are the branches. If you remain in me and I in you, you will bear much fruit; apart from me you can do nothing. If you do not remain in me, you are like a branch that is thrown away and withers; such branches are picked up, thrown into the fire and burned. If you remain in me and my words remain in you, ask whatever you wish, and it will be done for you. This is to my Father's glory, that you bear much fruit, showing yourselves to be my disciples. As the Father has loved me, so have I loved you. Now remain in my love. If you keep my commands, you will remain in my love, just as I have kept my Father's commands and remain in his love. I have told you this so that my joy may be in you and that your joy may be complete.

In Jeff Saturday's chapter, I mentioned that the desire to become a Christian icon became an idol for me; I wanted to be like Tony Dungy, Kurt Warner, or the Tim Tebow of today. But that's not abiding in Christ. That's selfish. Just now, I admitted that there have been times when I've finished preaching a message and wanted to reward myself. Same thing. That's not remaining connected to the vine. That's self-promoting.

This passage boldly states that apart from Christ, we can do nothing of eternal value. There is an inability to produce spiritual fruit. There's an impotence of influence. If you're an advocate of the jersey effect, how scary is that? You may have a desire to make a positive impact and use your jersey for good, but if Christ isn't in the forefront of your intentions, your impact is going to be watered down and potentially useless. And that's why prayer is the linchpin behind the jersey effect. It keeps us, the branches, connected to Christ, the vine, and enables us to bear fruit. When we are continually connected to Christ through prayer, we see ourselves as valuable which enables us to see others as valuable.

Photo courtesy of the Indianapolis Colts

David Yonggi Cho is the pastor of the Yoido Full Gospel Church in Seoul, South Korea, the largest church congregation in the world with a million members (as of 2007). He wrote a book called *Prayer: Key to Revival*. In the book, he talks about how he'd wake up every morning at four o'clock and pray for four hours. Everyone asked him what the key to revival was, and prayer was his response.

Without prayer, we can do nothing. But with prayer, God can do *anything* through us. Prayer is our lifeline.

CHAPTER 9

REGGIE HODGES

COMPETITION: A MAN-MADE ENTERPRISE

Photo courtesy of the Indianapolis Colts

#2
Punter
Cleveland Browns
Height: 6' 0"
Weight: 220
Age: 30
Born: January 26, 1982, Champaign, Illinois
College: Ball State
Experience: 6 seasons (1 Rams, 1 Eagles,
1 Jets, 1 Titans, 2 Browns)
High School: Centennial High School,
Champaign, Illinois

"Adversity is the state in which man most easily becomes acquainted with himself, being especially free of admirers then." –John Wooden

To Reggie Hodges, Indianapolis Colts, punter

Reggie,

I still remember the first time I saw you punt the football. It was during training camp one year when I was injured. They brought you in to fill my spot while I was in rehab. Sitting on the turf watching your workout before they signed you was a fairly unsettling experience.

Oh sure, I'd been injured before. There were other punters in camp before when I was lame or just needed another leg to share the endless punting duties of an NFL training camp. Typically those punters were a very raw product with subpar leg strength. I didn't mind their company at all. In fact, sometimes I welcomed it. However, you were a very different "camp leg." You hit huge soaring punts—one after another.

You don't have to play very long in the NFL to perceive the "replacement phenomena"—that is, the day you get signed is the day someone starts working to replace you. It's how someone justifies their job in the front office. So I started feeling a twinge of insecurity. "Why is this guy so good ... and unsigned ... and here to 'relieve' me during my injury?" It didn't help anything when you walked up to me after your "bomb fest" workout and said something like, "Hunter, it is so nice to meet you, man. I want you to know I've been watching film of you for years. I've learned so much from you and your technique."

I think I smiled and said thanks, but inside I was probably thinking, Yeah, yeah, glad I could help, big fella ... just don't learn so much that they run me out of here for a newer model. *It was my first battle with this aspect of my sinful nature. Don't get me wrong; I had felt threatened and insecure many times before. But I usually just succumbed to these and responded with typical worldly responses—that is, anger, manipulation, competition, or thoughts like,* Oh yeah? Well I'll kick your @#$.

But with you, something different was happening. I wasn't surrendering to the usual emotions and responses. Sure, they were

*whispering in my ear, but something else was speaking to my heart.
It seemed very unnatural at the time. Indeed it was! God was using
this scenario with you to overhaul a very broken down part of my
character.*

*By the end of that training camp God had taught me a very
important lesson. Discipleship is more important than my job.
The kingdom of God is more important than my career. You, my
friend, are the person God used to open my eyes to just how much of
ourselves we are to give. I've watched men in the NFL for years play
the "friendly" game with those they compete against for a job. When
most of these men have their backs against the wall, you see who they
really love. They love themselves. I have done it with the best of them.
With absolute humility I am able to say that after our training camp
together (and the one the next year ... yeah, someone really liked
you), I was full of a genuine love for you and a concern for your life
and career. Little did I know that time would find us being friends
and brothers for life. There clearly isn't enough time here to speak of
our journey and all God has done along the road.*

*Watching you grow and develop as a man has been one of the
greatest joys of my life. The husband, father, friend, evangelist,
disciple maker, and professional you are humbles and challenges
me. Well, all these years later, having watched you walk with God
over exhilarating peaks, through tumultuous valleys, and across long
stretches of the "in-between," I can say with integrity that you have
added as much or more to my faith as I have to yours.*

*All I can say is that I am so glad I pulled that groin muscle
during training camp.*

Thanks for being faithful,

Hunter

Reggie Remembers

Suddenly, I understood what life was all about …

Now, my chapter is unique in the sense that while I was on the 2006 Colts training camp team, I wasn't on the team when they won the Super Bowl. Now I'm a punter for the Cleveland Browns.

I'm glad God brought me to Indianapolis nonetheless. Even though I was only there for training camp, it changed my life forever. My life was in the pits when I arrived in Indy. I was drafted by the St. Louis Rams in the sixth round out of Ball State University … then cut in week 6 … picked up by the Rams in week 13 … then cut again at the end of the season … earned a job with the Philadelphia Eagles the following season … then cut after three games.

My football résumé was pathetic enough, but my personal life, sadly, was the exact same way. Coming out of Ball State University, I wasn't at all prepared for the NFL. I wasn't ready for the fame. I wasn't ready for the money. I wasn't ready for the work ethic. And it destroyed me physically and emotionally. After I was cut from the Rams, I came home and bawled my eyes out. I felt like my entire world had come crashing down. I let my fiancée down. I let my family down. I let my supporters at Ball State down. And now I was a nobody because I no longer had football.

For the next six weeks, all I did was feel sorry for myself. Like I said, it was pathetic. The Rams brought me back on at the end of the season; then they cut me (again), and I did the exact same thing. I sat around, drank, and didn't take care of my body. I was an emotional wreck. This time, I gained thirty pounds. I don't know what was wrong with me. Perhaps it was culture shock. Sure, it wasn't Ball State anymore. Sure, I was in the same locker room as Marshall Faulk. But what did I expect? This was the *NFL*. I expected to simply stand out because of talent, like I did at Ball State. It was as if I had never worked for anything before. I just expected it to be given to me.

Whatever the case, I was running my life into the ground. Not only was I emotionally imploding, but financially, I was also struggling. Blown away by the money I was making in the league initially, I recklessly spent it like I'd be making that same money for the rest of my life, expecting to play all season with the Rams, and even expecting to have a long, flourishing career in the NFL. That offseason, my fiancée and I were broke, and I had no source of income.

My woes continued. I went to Philadelphia my second season in the league and beat out four guys for the punting job, hoping to make Philly my long-term place. I punted well my first game; then I punted terribly against Washington and punted even worse against the New York Giants, yielding a blocked punt because I didn't get it off in time. After three games, they cut me, and I went back to loathing myself and spending money I didn't have.

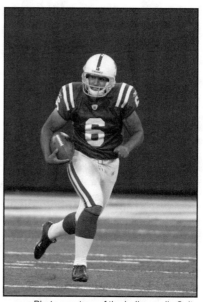

Luckily, from a financial standpoint, the Colts picked me up for training camp, but more importantly, from a spiritual standpoint, I ended up right where I needed to be—in Indy with Hunter.

Now, I knew I didn't have a future with the Colts. I had simply been brought on to relieve Hunter

Photo courtesy of the Indianapolis Colts

from an injury that he experienced in training camp. I was well aware he was one of the top five punters in the NFL. I was simply temporary. Still, my experience hopping from team to team showed me that a lot of players are peeved and sensitive whenever a team brings someone else in to challenge them. Even if there isn't a chance in the world they're going to be replaced, players typically try to intimidate new arrivals and make it clear that they shouldn't get too comfortable in *their* city. Hunter wasn't like that.

Hunter gave me a warm welcome I didn't expect. Within a couple days of my arrival in Indianapolis, he already asked if he could pray with me and gave me his new Connersvine album—something that would end up pulling me through some tough times in my life. Most importantly, he was speaking to me through his actions. He may not have realized it at the time, but it clicked for me: this was the way life was supposed to be. He was living it. He was a true man of God. And I wanted that.

What am I doing with myself? I wondered. Here I was, barely surviving financially; swimming in a pool of self-pity every time I got cut; living with Arin, my fiancée; drinking like a frat boy at Ball State; and hardly working to become a better punter, expecting to have a successful career handed to me like everything else.

I had spent the last fifteen years hiding from the Lord, masking myself with drugs and alcohol. Hanging around Hunter all summer made me realize my purpose in the NFL: kick the ball well and lead men to Christ. My purpose was to use football as a ministry, something I'd never even considered. It was a spiritual renewal. As I opened my Bible, words suddenly began to jump off the page. I remember reading Romans in my hotel room—trying to understand the power of salvation, urged to flee from my sin, and challenged, for the first time, to work hard in life. God woke me up at the right time too. By this time, I had married Arin and we had a child on the way. It was time for me to step up as a man of God, lead my family, and provide for them through hard work and persistence. No more whining. No more drinking. No more feeling sorry for myself. It was time to get things done. It was time to step up.

So I did. I'd wake up at 6:00 a.m. for Colts workouts in the morning, wait tables at Battery Park Saloon in downtown Indy from 11:00 a.m. to 2:30 p.m., and then work at the YMCA from 4:30 to 9:30 p.m. When training camp started, I was actually prepared because I finally knew what it meant to work hard. I finally knew what it took to earn something. I competed hard with Hunter at training camp and punted the best I ever had … after all, I was actually trying to improve and taking my job seriously. Life started to piece itself together because my focus was finally right. It wasn't about me anymore; it was about being there for my wife and kid.

After the second preseason game, however, the Colts cut me. Not a surprise. Can't say I didn't see it coming. But the most difficult thing was leaving Hunter. I enjoyed our fellowship and finally had a role model in Christ who showed me what it was like to walk with the Lord. I didn't want to leave that.

My experience in Indy wasn't something I was about to forget. Because of Hunter, I knew what a man of God looked like. Now I had a purpose in the NFL and—more than that—a purpose on this earth and in this life. My time with the Colts changed me and deeply affected my ministry, as you'll see in the following pages. Hunter decided to put competition aside (after all, I was after *his* job) and embraced me as a brother in Christ—thus laying the foundation for my ministry and the impact God was going to have on my teammates through me.

This is how God molded me—through pain, transition, and confusion—into an advocate of the jersey, a refining process that started in Indianapolis when I came face-to-face with Christ.

Stepping Up

I was *the* man now. God helped me see that. I couldn't just sit around and expect change to happen. If I wanted money for my wife and newborn son, Christian, I had to work for it. I had to step up. As the man, I had to provide.

So I sold copy machines. I sold cars. I went to workouts, still trying to make it in the NFL. I even swallowed my pride and asked good friends for a substantial amount of money because, once again, we were behind on finances and overinvesting in an implausible NFL dream. I'm just thankful I have good friends.

After being cut by the Colts, we ended up moving back to Arin's hometown of Fort Wayne, Indiana. I suffered through selling copy machines, a job I hated, and also had workouts with the Dolphins and Falcons.

My trip to Atlanta was the worst. Not only did I get beat out but also lost my sales job in Fort Wayne. On the way back to northern Indiana, my boss called and said, "We can't have you traveling, and we need a consistent employee. We're going to have to let you go." I was devastated on both the field and my personal life, as I was forced to return home with *nothing* for my family. No football, which would have been a bonus. And no more copy machines, which was our source of income.

That summer, I went to a kicking combine and talked to a few scouts, including one from the Seattle Seahawks, but nothing came of it, and I returned to Fort Wayne and accepted a job as a car salesman. Surprisingly, I was good at it. I was salesman of the month four of the six months I worked there and sold a whole bunch of cars my very first month, which allowed Arin and me to get back on our feet again and live comfortably. Selling cars was difficult because I wasn't playing football, but at the same time, I just allowed my newfound passion for witnessing in the locker room to translate into witnessing in the work place—in this case, a tiny used car dealership in northeast Indiana. Just as I had to step up and work hard for my family, I also had to step up in a spiritual sense. I decided that no matter where I was—whether it was next to Marshall Faulk's locker, selling copy machines, or selling cars—God wanted to use me. My life was in his hands.

Sacrificing Identity

When summertime rolled around (the summer after the Colts won the Super Bowl), I was punting again … and more confident than ever. I had trained under one of the best punters in the league, Hunter Smith, and continued to work hard while I was a copy machine salesman and car salesman. I was confident I could compete with anybody and knew I could place a punt anywhere on the field. All I was waiting for was a chance.

My chance came when I worked out in Las Vegas and the Seahawks, who brought me on briefly the season before, finally signed me. Their punter, Ryan Plackemeier, was coming off a difficult year, and I felt like I had an extremely good shot at earning the job. Ryan and I, like Hunter and I, also had a solid relationship. We'd stay up at night, reading our

Bibles and talking about what God was doing in our lives, helping alleviate some of the awkward tension between two players competing for the same spot.

Before the preseason started, Ryan tore his pectoral muscle while working out, an injury that takes a substantial amount of recovery time. I felt bad for him. That wasn't the way I wanted to earn the job. But nonetheless, I had to be ready. I played well in the preseason and was positive they'd sign me on. I knew that I was finally going to make my return.

But it wasn't to be. The team went with Ryan anyway. And I was baffled. Don't get me wrong; I was happy for my dear friend, but I was also extremely confused. I thought Seattle was my big opportunity, and not only did I feel like I earned the job to begin with, but also they went with someone who was recovering from an injury over someone who was perfectly healthy.

I just remember going home and immediately getting on my knees, crying out to the Lord, saying, "What do you want from me? What am I not doing? I spend time with you. I study your Word. If you don't want me to play football, I'll be done."

I wasn't just speaking irrationally. I was serious. If God wanted me to go a different direction with my life, then that's what I was going to do.

So I gave it up.

Real Identity

"I'm not done with you here yet," I could almost hear God say it audibly. This wasn't the end. After I completely turned over my NFL dreams to God, I got a call from the New York Jets.

In New York, I had the best workout of my life. They picked me up in week 2 and told me that I was going to be their punter the remainder of the season. This time, football was the last thing on my mind. I cared about one thing: ministering to guys in the locker room, and that was it. Even when I pulled my hamstring early in the season and they brought in another punter, I remember not being fazed by that. My identity was no longer in football. It was in the Lord. And as much as I wanted to excel in New York, I knew God was going to use me wherever he took me. I understood that God was using all the junk and trials to draw me closer to him. As I wrestled with pride and idolatry, God was constantly showing me that I needed to be dependent on him. That's where true growth takes place—when our futures and identities are placed in God alone.

Photo courtesy of the Indianapolis Colts

The thing is it's easy to preach that, but it's harder to live it. And at the end of my season, after being on the Jets roster for thirteen weeks, the most successful NFL season I had, I was challenged, once again, to live out what I was preaching.

"Reg," my special teams coach said to me, "you won't be punting for us next year." Again, I was crushed, and I didn't understand it. It had been my best season yet. But I could still hear God telling me, "Keep ministering, keep ministering."

The Jets brought in five punters in the offseason. Do you know how rare it is for a team to bring in that many punters? They must've *really* wanted me out. But it didn't matter. I beat everyone out and punted great. I even punted exceptionally well in the preseason games. Sure, they wanted me out for whatever reason, but again, I earned my spot.

Or so I thought.

Not long after preseason, the Jets' general manager called me to his office. "We're letting you go," he told me.

I was distraught and frustrated; I asked, "Who is replacing me?"

"We don't know yet," he said.

That's the amazing thing about all of this. The Jets cut me before they even had a replacement for me. That was one of the hardest blows I took—not because my identity was still in football but because I still wanted to excel in football, first for my family but also for myself, and I had clearly earned my spot. Plus, on the home front, my wife hadn't moved to New York the season before, because she was afraid that would happen. So that was a whole NFL season of traveling back and forth to see Arin, Christian, and my baby daughter. I just wanted something consistent.

I was so confused, and I didn't know what to do. So I called Hunter. All Hunter did was listen and pray for me. He was *for* me. Around him, I could be vulnerable and candid. And at twenty-five, I broke down and cried.

Trials Strengthen Your Ministry

In 2009, I was picked up by the Tennessee Titans after Craig Hentrich blew out his calf. Arin decided to take a leap of faith and bring our family down with me. I had just spent an entire season with the Jets, and I should've spent more than that, so we both felt like I had decent job security … for at least a year. I finally had my foot in the door of the NFL.

My first game was against the Jets. And I punted great. If I'm being honest, that felt *really* good. I wanted to show them what they were missing out on, and I did. I also punted well the next game against Jacksonville. Arin decided to come down the third week I was on the team, which happened to be our bye week.

That Tuesday, the general manager called me into his office. "We're going to go a different direction," he told me. This was my *seventh* time getting cut from an NFL team.

I never want to relive that drive from the stadium to our new apartment, where my wife was helping our family get settled in. I was broken. I was crying. I was mad at myself. I was mad at God. I hated Tennessee. I hated New York. And most of all, I hated football. My son needed me, my daughter needed me, and my wife needed me—how could I explain this one? Arin took a leap of faith, and *this* is what happened. I sat in the driveway for forty-five minutes and then entered the house.

I just held her, loved her, and tried to remain strong.

Impact

"I don't know how long I'll be here," I told the chaplain at the Cleveland Browns, "but I want to be sure I have an effect on some men for however long I'm here."

The Browns picked me up after Tennessee, and it turned out to be a successful season. I ended up back with the Browns in 2010, where I had the best season of my career. I was in the top ten in every category and even in the top three in one category. This time, the Browns actually came to me and offered me an extended contract and signing bonus. To me, it was like God was saying, "You've stuck it out, and now I can trust you with this."

After my dreams had been crushed seven times, I finally signed a deal. I gave money to my parents, gave money to ministries, and told Arin that all I wanted to do was give the money away. It had been a good year for us, and it allowed me to experience a sense of normalcy in my family life for the first time, as they moved to Cleveland to join me. On top of that, I was doing what Hunter taught me to do. I was ministering to my teammates. That was my purpose. Football was secondary. All I cared about was bringing glory to God.

After the 2010 offseason, I returned to practice, and in a freak incident, I blew out my Achilles tendon, catching a high snap. It felt like someone hacked me in the ankle with a sledgehammer; my tendon rolled all the way up my calf. As I lay on the ground, I remember thinking, *I refuse to let this test affect my testimony. If these men who have seen me walk with the Lord all of a sudden see that circumstances rule me, I'll lose my opportunity to witness.* I wasn't worried about the 2011 season. I wasn't worried about who could potentially replace me. That didn't matter anymore. My main concern was following God, even if I was in pain. So we prayed right then and there on the field, and before the next game, all eighty-nine players bowed down in the locker room and prayed for my leg. One of my teammates said that was the only time he'd ever seen everyone take a knee like that to lift *one* person up in prayer. Perhaps they knew it was prayer that I'd appreciate the most. I don't know. God uses trials to magnify your ministry; therefore, embrace your trials.

I can't wait for what trial comes next.

HUNTER REFLECTS

When Reggie Hodges came to the Colts' front door, I had a decision to make. I was injured, and even though I'd been with the Colts for a while, as a punter, you always feel like your job is in jeopardy. Punters, unlike franchise players like Peyton Manning and Dwight Freeney, are very replaceable. All I

> *God uses trials to magnify your ministry; therefore, embrace your trials.*

do is kick a stupid ball. And whenever *any* backup player is brought on for *any* position, the player who is being challenged oftentimes treats the newcomer with disdain and aggravation. If I'm being honest, I wanted to treat Reggie like that. I'd been with the Colts for almost a decade, and this was *my* team. I didn't care that I was injured. I still didn't like the concept of someone challenging me and my livelihood.

But I had a choice to make. I could either embrace the world's standards of competition and treat Reggie like so many other NFL players treat their potential replacements, or I could accept him. Would I go with my fleshly tendencies? Or would I love him?

It wasn't easy, but I decided to go with the latter. I sat and watched film with him. I taught him a type of punt called the "rugby ball." And I even found myself injured on the sideline, hoping he'd be successful and praising him when he did well. My flesh wanted to say, "I hope he shanks it. I hope he shanks it." But I made a conscious decision to strive after Christ and not conform to the pattern of the world ... which is fueled by competition.

When I played for Washington, I had a similar relationship with Sam Paulescu, who replaced me in 2009 when I was injured and missed three games. We hung out together. We had fun together. There wasn't as much discipleship as there was with Reggie and me, but we were still good friends. And when I was cut in 2010, Sam was the only player whom the Redskins phoned to replace me. I called him the day after I got cut and congratulated him on getting the job. It wasn't easy. Nor was it easy to initially welcome Reggie. But the Holy Spirit convicted me that—although it would be conceived as countercultural and radical—it was what I was supposed to do. It was the godly response.

One night, in a particular moment of wrestling with the Lord, I sensed God whispering this truth to my heart: "I have not called you to be a competitor. I've called you to be a warrior." See, competition is for earthly trophies. Being a warrior is for a kingdom. Competition for earthly purposes is meaningless. But if you're a warrior, you're fighting for something that has lasting value.

> *Competition is for earthly trophies. Being a warrior is for a kingdom.*

We are part of a culture where being competitive is a virtue. Competition, though permissible, is not an adequate means to glorify God in itself. God will never be pleased with one's desire or ability to assert one's own dominance over another. It is simply contrary to his nature. He is, however, pleased when we truly work at our craft with pure hearts to love him and glorify him, *not* to be better than the other guy.

Romans 12:1–2 states, "Therefore, I urge you, brothers and sisters, in view of God's mercy, to offer your bodies as a living sacrifice, holy and pleasing to God—this is your true and proper worship. Do not conform to the pattern of this world, but be transformed by the renewing of your mind. Then you will be able to test and approve what God's will is—his good, pleasing and perfect will."

We're told to not conform to this world. We live in a society fueled by competition. In America, it's all about winning. It's about being on top. Capitalism is not bad; I think it's made us an incredible nation because we push one another and challenge one another. But I'm also convinced that our capitalistic mindset tends to intrude on our Christianity. And instead of supporting one another, even when we are being competed against, we put ourselves first. It hurts our ministry because witnessing *can't* be self-centered. And unfortunately, that's what competition can do. It makes you think about one thing: your own well-being. It makes you think about your own importance—how you deserve this and that. Seeing Reggie as a valuable son of God whom Christ died for helped me transition from a worldly perspective to a much larger spiritual perspective. Through value, God took our relationship to an entirely different level.

Competition is a pattern of this world. Putting others down to elevate yourself is also a pattern of this world. We are called not to conform to this world but rather be transformed in Christ. Plus, it's a much more stress-free way to live. If God is in control of my future, then I don't have to worry about competing. All I have to do is give my all and be a warrior. All I have to do is love people … even if they're fighting for my job. That's what God has called us to do, and we need to do it.

Photo courtesy of the Indianapolis Colts

John 3:30 is only eight words long, but it's radical in our culture: "He must become greater; I must become less" (NIV). John the Baptist, though the center of attention and attraction, understood what his role was. He was paving the way for the Lord, and he needed to decrease so the Lord could be elevated in the process. That's what we're called to do. We must decrease as we exalt Christ in our relationships.

Another passage that *must* be mentioned regarding competition is Matthew 18:1–4, which says, "At that time the disciples came to Jesus and asked, 'Who, then, is the greatest in the kingdom of heaven?' He called a little child to him, and placed the child among them. And he said: 'Truly I tell you, unless you change and become like little children, you will never enter the kingdom of heaven. Therefore, whoever takes the lowly position of this child is the greatest in the kingdom of heaven.'"

Just the nature of the question "Who is the greatest?" implies selfish ambition among the disciples. The disciples wanted to compete against one another, but Jesus, in a nutshell, says that competition doesn't exist in the kingdom of God. Competition means striving to defeat someone. But the truth is that you can't follow Christ *and* try to make yourself great. They don't go together. So Jesus responds by discussing relationships and the community of the kingdom. In the kingdom, they are supposed to watch out for one another. They are supposed to support one another—not compete against each other.

Look at Reggie's testimony, quite possibly the most up-and-down story in this book, marred with scars and tribulations. But look at the impact he has had. Look at the way God has used trials to magnify Reggie's ministry. And it amazes me to think that his life transformation might have never taken place—that the transformation he's seen in the men he has discipled might never have taken place—if I had acted on my selfish mindset in an attempt to compete with him and scare him away.

Look what God can do when we conform to *his* ways and choose to be warriors for *his* kingdom.

CHAPTER 10

JUSTIN SNOW

Free Pass: Corrupting Influence

Photo courtesy of the Indianapolis Colts

#48
Long snapper
Indianapolis Colts
Height: 6' 3"
Weight: 240
Age: 35
Born: December 21, 1976, Fort Worth, Texas
College: Baylor
Experience: 12 seasons (Colts)
High School: Cooper High School,
Abilene, Texas

"Character is much easier kept than recovered." –Thomas Paine

To Justin Snow, Super Bowl champion, Indianapolis Colts, long snapper

Justin,

Maybe it shouldn't be so funny to me. But it is.

One of my favorite hilarious memories (of many) from our career together with the Colts involves the guy who is responsible for hiring us. The great thing about this memory is that it is "the gift that keeps on giving all year long." Or, to be sure, about seven years long.

It took Bill Polian seven years to learn your name. Now, I understand how hard it is to learn names on an NFL football team. I can confuse (or forget) names and faces with the best of them. There is so much turnover in personnel that it can be hard to keep up. However, you might think that our President and General Manager would know the first name of his four-year ... five-year ... six-year ... seven-year veteran deep snapper. You might think—but you would be wrong. You have had lots of nicknames over the years (Snow, Snowflake, Snowman, J-Snow, J-Sweet, 4 Tone, etc.) But ... my personal favorite was Bill's.

Josh.

Not a nickname at all. Just the wrong dad gum name.

So, whether it was within the halls of the Colts training facility, or on the practice field, or at the RCA Dome, or Lucas Oil Stadium, or Gillette Stadium in New England, or the team plane coming home, you were Josh ... for seven years!

"Good luck, Josh."

"Go get 'em, Josh."

"Great job, Josh"

"Hey, Josh! Come here for a second."

"Congratulations, Josh."

Or, my personal favorite, when passing each other in the halls of the facility:

Justin: "Hi Mr. Polian."

Bill: "Josh."

Just the name...with a warm, grandfatherly smile. That's all. Classic.

(Bill, if you're reading this don't be mad at Justin. This was all my idea.)

You might wonder why I've chosen to spend so much time on this story in this letter. Well ... because it's funny. I have been laughing out loud many times while writing it. However, humor isn't the sole purpose.

You and I have walked through a lot of life together. It is overwhelming for me to try and encapsulate my description of our friendship and my appreciation of who you are into a few words. So I won't. But I will say this.

People who come to God sometimes take years to learn who they really are in him. It has been a long journey for me. It has been the same for you. I'll never forget the day you stuck your massive finger in Chris Polian's chest and told him, "You tell your dad that I'm tired of him calling me Josh. My name is Justin Snow."

It was a stake in the ground for you. You were fed up with the wrong identifier. Likewise, there have been many moments for you spiritually where the same thing has happened. Looking back on the landscape of our friendship it has been a privilege to watch you confront evil in your own life and say, "No, that's not who I am." I know you aren't perfect. But, you see your need for him who is perfect. You see the need to let God identify you correctly in the face of a world constantly trying to call you by the wrong name. He has remade and renamed you, brother. That is most important.

It has been a miraculous thing to watch you grow in your relationship with God. There was a time when I wondered (as many wondered about me at one point) if you were ever gonna "get it." It is hard to be young and wealthy. It is hard to be handsome and successful. It is hard to be strong in the world's eyes and finally come to grips with the reality that you are weak without God. You have realized this and are a stronger Christian, husband, father, friend, and teammate for it.

It is a privilege to walk with you brother.

Thanks Justin, (Bill, take note.)

Hunter

Justin Remembers

It was a Friday night. I was driving my black Escalade. And I had two other Colts players in the SUV with me, along with three women we had just picked up from Broad Ripple, Indy's hippest bar scene. I had been drinking; I shouldn't have been driving, but I still drove anyway.

That's when the unimaginable happened. A policeman turned on his lights, as he tailed me in his car. Back to reality.

Up to this point, I went through life thinking that I was invincible. I thought I was special. Nothing could faze me. Nothing could stop me from doing whatever I wanted to do … even if it was dangerous. I was in my midtwenties at the start of my career in Indianapolis (I've been there since 2000), and this was my mindset at the time.

My first mistake was that I was driving, obviously. My second mistake was that I pulled into someone's driveway instead of pulling over to the side of the road. I was in trouble. I gripped the steering wheel, and my career flashed before my eyes. It felt like an eternity as the cop walked up to my parked SUV.

I began to think about the possible consequences. I was playing for the *Colts*. They don't put up with foolishness like this. They don't tolerate sketchy behavior. That wasn't how they built their organization. *My career in Indianapolis is over,* I thought to myself.

And it was all because I was careless, flirting with destruction and nearly forfeiting the blessings God had poured upon me.

The officer looked at me.

"Sir," I said.

He studied me.

"Hmmm … we were looking for someone else in a black Escalade."

I looked at him. Was he serious?

"Well, you aren't the guy," he said. "But next time, don't pull into someone's driveway."

Then he left.

I couldn't believe it. For some reason, God decided to protect me, and he didn't have to. I was the one who was messing up. I was the one throwing my life away. I was the one who deserved to be punished for my actions. I was the one who wasn't following after him. But for whatever reason, he protected me. And I'll never know why, for sure.

After that, I knew I had to shape up. Spirituality aside, I knew my actions weren't intelligent even from a worldly standpoint. I almost messed up my career, tainted my good name, and damaged my otherwise clean reputation. Yes, I know that people drive after drinking. It happens. And a lot of times, they make it home just fine. But then there are the statistics.

Photo courtesy of the Indianapolis Colts

There are those who kill people. Those who ruin their lives. Those who can't find a job because it's always on their record. I didn't want to be a statistic. I didn't want to keep playing with fire.

But that's exactly what the NFL does to some athletes. It makes you believe you are your own god. Success makes you believe that you're the center of the world and you're invincible. Whenever I went out, my drinks were free. My meals were free. I didn't have to chase girls, because they chased me. All because I played football for the Colts. And before you know it, you're into the money, the women, and all of the material things the devil throws at you.

The NFL lifestyle snatched me during my early years in the league. I was blown away by the money, and I went down the common road of destruction that Matthew 7:13 talks about: "For the gate is wide and the way is easy that leads to destruction, and those who enter by it are many" (NASB). Money and greed are home runs for the devil ... and Satan got me. I was boneheaded. I was stubborn. But luckily, even though I was going out every Friday night to the clubs, I had Christian teammates in the locker room who were pursuing me and praying for me—like Hunter Smith; Jeff Saturday; and our chaplain, Eric Simpson.

I didn't grow up in the church. My brother had cerebral palsy, and my family never made it a priority to attend service on Sunday because we were "too busy" taking care of him. But I *was* introduced to Christ at a young age because I attended youth group functions and went on church trips with my friends. I wanted what they had and was exposed to the gospel.

Success makes you believe that you're the center of the world and you're invincible.

When I got to college, I was a knucklehead. I was into the party scene and drifting from my faith. But then my brother died. That hit home for me. That's when I started getting involved with a group of men for a Bible study and accountability. I really depended on God during that time. I was no longer going to parties, hooking up with women, and cheating on my tests. I was on fire for Christ.

By the time I got to the Colts, I was beginning to slip down that exact same path I tumbled down in college. There's something about the perks of the NFL that are so appealing, especially when the attractions of this world are thrown at you at such a young age. It was just so easy. Again, it took a strong group of guys in accountability and fellowship to unlock the shackles that the NFL lifestyle had on me. I realized that I was at a point in my career where I needed to grow up. I was going out to experience the nightclubs and the drinking, but I needed to leave it behind. I met Heather, who would soon become my wife, and with the help of our group that was striving after Christ, I was convicted by the Holy Spirit that I needed to change.

Two of the greatest people in my spiritual journey were Hunter Smith and Eric Simpson. I'll never forget their impact on me. They were there from the beginning and saw me grow as a Christian. They helped pull me away from the party-on-Friday-night lifestyle and helped me mature in my faith. We had a group that met twice a week for prayer, Bible study, and fellowship. That accountability was instrumental in my journey. Finally, thanks to those guys, I was in a position to grow. I got married, and on December 5, 2005, Hunter baptized me, thus declaring publicly that my former lifestyle was over. I've been walking with the Lord since—not to say I haven't fallen or sinned or struggled, but I'm trying.

Unfortunately, a lot of guys who have been corrupted by the NFL lifestyle don't turn their lives around. They're still pursuing nothingness and searching for fulfillment in bars, in nightclubs, and in the bedroom. Their souls have been poisoned by the charms of this world.

That's what the NFL can do.

HUNTER REFLECTS

Gradually, most people become less and less the center of attention. This is the system by which most people grow up and learn to make it in the world on their own. This is not always the case with NFL athletes.

In fact, I would say it rarely is the case.

Athletics offer young people many things. As they enter adolescence, athletics offer many experiences: exercise, teamwork, camaraderie, and discipline. Sports also offer attention to them. And it can be a lot of attention. Public sporting events offer the purest form of attention. There is a *crowd* surrounding a field with *players* who are the *focus*. This focus is something most athletes grow accustomed to and become fond of at an early age.

When young athletes start receiving attention in their lives, they will inevitably start to pay more attention to themselves as well. After all, everyone else focuses on them (parents/coaches/fans), so why shouldn't they? Especially in our society, where some parents have lost their minds over youth sports. Many parents think their kid is going to be a big-time athlete.

The result of this pattern of development in a young Christian athlete's life can be the gradual hijacking of any good he hopes to accomplish through his platform. They may have initially felt a call from God to do great things and reach the high places of culture through the language of athletics, but their intentions are often poisoned by self, just like Justin shared.

Early on in my life, I wanted to use my position to fulfill the greatest commandments, "Love God" and "Love others." However, the only love modeled in our society has been love of self. So when success comes and the platform has been built, many Christian athletes use their status to love themselves.

Oh, the excuses we make! We are *so* important that we always seem too busy or tired or whatever for what we originally felt called to. As a result, our original motivation to love God is reduced in action to an annual publicized trip to a hospital or an appearance at some fancy two-hundred-dollars-a-plate fundraiser where the focus is *us*. It is just too little, too late.

As Justin says, that's just what the NFL can do to you. It's infectious. It's dangerous. It's something you need to be prepared for. But it's not just the NFL; it's athletics in general. It's *anything* that results in a significant amount of attention on yourself. And perhaps the root of it is the "free pass" mentality.

Photo courtesy of the Indianapolis Colts

In reality, athletes oftentimes receive special treatment and preference that allows them to shirk the responsibility that was God-given. It's as if some players equate God's favor on their lives with special favors they receive because of their status as a professional athlete. They got it wrong. To whom much is given, much is expected. It's more about living up to God's expectations, rather than the expectations of men—which can end up showering prominent people with favors.

You see, football teams need both a passing game and a running game. People often talk about teams that have one but not the other. There is another game a lot of players don't like to talk about, however. It's the "free pass" that comes from your fame and the "running game" you play by running away from responsibility.

> *It's more about living up to God's expectations, rather than the expectations of men—which can end up showering prominent people with favors.*

Let me give a scenario that comes from the real life experience of athletes. I was struggling in a science class and decided to talk to the teacher. The science teacher responded, "Hunter, you take care of the football, and I will take care of your grade." Now, as a kid I walked away thinking, *Cool, this is a great solution to studying!*

After years of free passes, free dinners, free tickets to concerts, favors, and front-row seats, an athlete can hardly help but develop an attitude of "free passes." You start thinking, *Everyone likes me, everyone wants to do favors for me, and I deserve the special treatment that comes with sports.* Our culture shapes the mindset of the athlete into believing, "You take care of the football, and we'll take care of you." And since everyone likes me and understands I should get a free pass, surely God wants to give me a free pass, too. Like a lot of things in life, our experiences shape our theology and affect our view of God.

A friend of mine who is a genuine Christian experienced a free pass in college. He was struggling to make the grades but at six feet six, weighing 310 pounds, with 8 percent body fat, his degree was practically handed to him when he enrolled. He went in to see a teacher about some credits he needed and was helped out big time because he was an athlete. The sad part of his story is what happened at the next stage of his life. He was so accustomed to free passes that when he was drafted by an NFL team, he struggled because he actually had to work—kind of like Reggie's initial struggle coming out of Ball State.

Thankfully for this friend, his story didn't end in defeat. Later on, in his thirties, he caught his stride and started doing well in life. He's a great Christian, he has a beautiful family, and even though the early years were a struggle, he has another career now and learned to work hard ... even for things that didn't come naturally like football did.

Sadly, there are so many athletes who don't get their lives in order after all those free passes. They struggle after their sports careers because they literally do not know how to make it. They aren't accustomed to the work ethic and relentless determination that is required to be successful in the real world.

This friend is an example of a success story of an NFL player who went on and found his way in life after all the free passes. Guys like this play a short time in the league, make $1.25 to $1.5 million, and often end up bankrupt and divorced. Thankfully, that was not his story.

Don't let it be your story either. Don't buy into the culture of the free pass, because it will eventually wear down your character.

Even now, I don't pay for as many things as I should. I get offered all kinds of free dinners, tickets to events, and other perks. And this weaves into a part of my personal experience with God. I spent years viewing God the way I viewed everybody else. I thought that he might not completely approve of my lifestyle, but he certainly was happy to just grin and bear my lifestyle if I was willing to stand up for him as an athlete. Because everyone treated me like I was more important, I subconsciously believed God saw me as more important. As blasphemous as it sounds, I believed I was an asset to God, which enabled him to better accomplish his purposes. It happened because many authority figures in my life gave me that pattern of thinking.

When you have teachers just giving you grades you didn't earn, it's difficult not to transfer that mindset to God. You begin to think that God will take care of you, too, no matter what you're doing in your spiritual walk. So I found myself thinking, *God must like me, and surely he will give me a free pass on some pet sins in my life.*

If you have an adequate understanding of the holiness of God, a fear of the Lord, and a real understanding of who Jesus is at a young age, you won't be sidelined in life by a crippling mindset of the free pass. If your roots are in the biblical Jesus, if you have received biblical salvation, that will change the way you view all of the perks and the way people see you.

Now I will say this: most of the guys I know in the NFL are really hard workers. There is a level of success in sports that weeds out those who are coasting. And I've noticed that the older a player gets, the harder they work. It's because you know you are getting close to the end of it all, and you want to make it last. This requires hard work. And all that hard work develops into success, which leads to more free passes. So I don't want to send the wrong message here. The free perks aren't necessarily an issue coming from a desire to not work hard, but the free perks can develop a mindset in an athlete that distorts his view of who he is and where his true value comes from.

At one stage of my education, I was forced to take Calculus. I had previously taken Algebra II but struggled significantly. It was my weakest subject, and there was no way I could grasp it. It would have taken God's Holy Spirit literally filling my head with answers and physically taking my hand to work out the test problems. I was a cowboy and a quarterback—not a math-

Photo courtesy of the Indianapolis Colts

ematician. I didn't know anything about the x and y intercepts. I knew Xs and Os and, occasionally, interceptions.

Now, take algebra's challenges and multiply it by xyz, and you've got a deplorable subject called Calculus, something, I assure you, is straight from the pits of hell. I failed all three tests and the final in Calculus. And when I say I failed, I don't mean 65 percent. I'm talking about much lower than that. Take a thermometer, for example. My grades would have been below freezing.

When my Calculus final was over, I walked up to my teacher and said, "Hey, listen, I failed all three tests, and I know I just failed your final. Do you have any idea what is about to happen? Am I going to have to quit playing football?"

His response was, "You'll be fine."

"I don't know if you understand," I said. "My name is Hunter, and I failed three tests and the final in your class. I need to know if there is anything I can do to make this right."

Again, he looked at me and said, "You'll be fine."

"Welp, okay then," I said, turning around and joyfully whistling down the hallway. This is the difficult thing in all of this. I was on the borderline of becoming a whole class behind, but my teacher looked at me, a mathematical dunce, dead in the eyes and said, "You'll be fine."

He ended up giving me a D, which I'd say was probably for my effort on homework … if anything. But still, does anybody deserve to pass a class in which they failed three tests and a final? Probably not. And there is no doubt in my mind I received a passing grade solely because I was on the football team. My message to you as an athlete is a warning that you will face experiences like this—experiences that test the very core of your being. So keep your focus on who you really are and where your value comes from.

What the free pass does is make you self-seeking because you realize all that you can get, which, in the end, makes you selfish. The free pass makes you believe and trust in your own importance. The cross, on the other hand, allows you to see your true value in Christ—which extinguishes self-importance because you humbly come to the realization that you're nothing without Christ, that without Christ you'd be in hell, and that you don't deserve anything because you're a sinful man and a wretch. Romans 2:6–8 speaks directly about selfishness: "He will render to each one according to his works: to those who by patience in well-doing seek for glory and honor and immortality, he will give eternal life; but for those who are self-seeking and do not obey the truth, but obey unrighteousness, there will be wrath and fury" (ESV).

These temptations, however, are our crosses to bear as athletes. And the first step to bearing that cross and destroying these temptations is recognizing the potential destruction. Luke 9:23–25 states, "Then he said to them all: 'Whoever wants to be my disciple must deny themselves and take up their cross daily and follow me. For whoever wants to save their life will lose it, but whoever loses their life for me will save it. What good is it for someone to gain the whole world, and yet lose or forfeit their very self?'" (NIV). Throughout history, people have made the mistake of "selling themselves" to their career, to their talent, to money, or to something else that eventually flees from them. People go from the hope of their professional career, to the despair of it being over, to the destruction of their personal lives. This is not new to our generation. When you lose that thing in your life that defines you, you will feel completely lost. I think this is why the Bible states so strongly that Jesus came to save those who were "lost." It is through him who we must find our identity, our strength, and our significance. Our playing careers always come to a close, but God has a plan for our lives.

It's a mindset, however, that must be combated—a self-seeking, career-centered, worldly, appetizing lifestyle that seeks to destroy. As you've read in this book, it's tried to destroy just about everyone. And it'll destroy you too … if you let free passes run their course.

CHAPTER 11

TONY DUNGY

THE JERSEY EFFECT ACCORDING TO TONY

Photo courtesy of the Indianapolis Colts

Author of the best-selling books *Quiet Strength*, *Uncommon*, and *The Mentor Leader*
NBC Sunday Night Football commentator
Former head coach of the Super Bowl XLI champion Indianapolis Colts

"Be sure you put your feet in the right place, then stand firm."

–Abraham Lincoln

To Tony Dungy, Super Bowl champion, Indianapolis Colts, head coach

Tony,

I have a few reasons for writing this letter. First and foremost, life has taught me that if you have something to say, you should say it now because the future is very uncertain. All of the other reasons pretty much flow out of the first, so I'll just get to the point here.

I came from Texas, where football is first (as you know). My town was one of those places where the varsity football playbook was applied at all levels of football, starting in early middle school. We had a great coach and a winning tradition with a lot of players who went on to play college ball and a disproportionate amount (relative to our town's size) who have played in the NFL. You coached two of them, Charlie Johnson and me. From there I experienced the Lou Holtz Show at Notre Dame, along with a couple of years under Bob Davie. After that, it was Jim Mora, yourself, Jim Zorn, and Mike Shanahan. This is not about me and my experiences with coaches, though. This is about you.

The NFL has been an instrument in the hand of God to teach me many lessons. Most of them have dealt with the inherent wickedness and selfishness of the world. The league is a flagship for the world and its values. I must admit that I often felt uncomfortable and out of place within the confines of an NFL career. I struggled with idolatry, greed, insecurity, pride, and the list goes on. I am writing this letter to tell you that of all the people I have been coached by or played with along my football journey, you have shown the most devotion to the Lord. Celebrity status, wealth, and fame are storms to be weathered for Christians, and your life continually shines through the clouds. You have challenged and inspired me time and again to keep being a light in a dark world. Your life is a testimony to the faithfulness and power of God.

I will never forget those instances where we would be standing on the sidelines in practice, talking about your books and my music. You were so interested in how songs are written. In particular, I recall a song off our Connersvine album called "A Time to Die" that was really interesting to you. I always thought that was cool because it didn't get a lot of acclaim from anyone else, but it is, in my opinion, probably one of the best songs I've ever written. It was special to me that it stood out to you. Before long, ten or fifteen minutes would pass, and you still wanted to talk about music. I would look out on the field and think, Wow. Peyton Manning is out there running 7-on-7. Coaches are screaming. Players are working. An NFL practice is happening, and the head coach is interested in my dinky music career. *That meant a lot to me, and it still does. No other coach I've been around has ever been that interested in anything in my life outside of how I could help the team win more games. You weren't in a hurry, weren't worried about looking like you were working or saving your job. You were just interested in somebody else's life and willing to take the time to listen.*

It was this nuance of your godly character that changed the culture of the Indianapolis Colts. Your leadership and authentic interest in other people is simple obedience to Jesus' commandment "Love your neighbor." Your obedience to that commandment is just a by-product of your love for God. A man who loves God and other people is a man who changes the world. That's what God used you to do with the Indianapolis Colts. Sure, you've written books, spoken to thousands, and had many other great public/media exploits for the kingdom. Those are authentic and world-changing. However, I'll remember you walking around the practice field in the heat of a training camp morning, with a list of notable things from that morning's one-year Bible reading. While the management was trying to decide whom to cut and whom to keep, while the players were tense and trying to make the team, while the world was playing out its cruel, self-centered process on a hundred yards of freshly chalked turf, you were approaching different coaches and players to talk about God's Word. All of this while being a diligent Xs and Os man who never neglected his primary professional responsibility to field a winning team and who, in fact, coached the winningest team in NFL history over a decade's time. Oh yeah, and won a Super Bowl championship. I took note of your balance and priorities along the way. I will not forget what I saw.

This letter would be too long if I brought to light all of the times I witnessed and experienced Jesus in your life over the years, but I'm grateful for the impact you've had on my life. I hope Oregon is beautiful and Eric is watching the ball in, tucking it away, and getting up field.

In Christ,

Hunter

TONY REMEMBERS

I could tell you about the Super Bowl, but most of it you've probably already heard. I want to describe to you what the jersey effect means to me and share some personal experiences that shaped me as I learned how to wear the jersey and in turn taught my players. My chapter in this book is different in the sense that I'm not telling my story—you've already heard it—but I'm writing about what the jersey effect means to me and what the jersey effect can mean in your life. My thoughts are directed more specifically toward athletes, but I do believe they hold truth for all walks of life.

Growth in Four Areas

Time and time again, I have seen an athlete's faith hijacked. And the hijacker is what Christ calls "the cares of the world." Obvious distractions are money, fame, and pursuing success. But it's not always those vices that draw our attention away from God's plans. A lot of times it's things like trying to take care of your family, taking care of your home, and providing for your future. They are good things, yet still a distraction. Other times, it's the realization that God has given you a special talent, and you feel the need to work at that talent ... all the time. Again, working hard is good but still a distraction. You can be in your football career and fall in love and marry someone and start your family. Still, a distraction. Maybe you realize you're on a great team that has the potential to win a national championship or you're on an NFL team that could make it to the Super Bowl this season. Still, a distraction. All of these, though positive things, are still "cares of the world." And it's essential that you keep your desire to be used by God at the forefront of your mind and intentions. Though God doesn't frown on us working hard in our careers, or working for our families, or working for a Super Bowl, he does frown when those things become our gods.

If I could sit down with you and look you in the eyes, this is the advice I would give: You need to try to grow in four ways—academically, athletically, socially, and spiritually. Unfortunately, in our country, we tend to focus on one or two of these areas and ignore the others. The sad part is that you will hear a lot of emphasis from our culture on your athletic development first. It's not wrong to grow athletically, because you certainly want to capitalize on the athletic talents that God has given you. But it can't stand alone.

Photo courtesy of the Indianapolis Colts

Do you have the same amount of desire to grow academically? My guess is probably not. Understand that your academic growth is more important than your athletic growth. How you grow academically is going to be longer-lasting in its impact; it stretches far beyond the athletic prime you attain in your midtwenties. Are you willing to put the equal effort into academics that you put into athletics? Often it's hard to spend the time on academics because you don't see the payoff right away.

And it's not emphasized in our society as much as athletic development, but I want you to know that it's more important. Believe it.

Another area you must not ignore is the area of social growth. Make friends who are good for you—who can sharpen you—who will make you a better person. Understand that the friends you choose will help you grow into the person God has designed you to become. They'll help shape your life positively, and you'll be able to encourage them in the same way.

But the greatest question is, "Are you developing spiritually?" It's crucial that your answer is yes. Unfortunately, people don't emphasize enough the spiritual development of athletes, especially the spiritual development of boys. If you are growing in the first three areas—athletically, academically, and socially—and feel like you've got it made … you really don't. You are missing the most important area of all. I talk to athletes all the time who wake up and realize that though they've had outstanding careers, they feel empty inside. There is a gaping hole in their lives. Something is missing. Even though they have excelled athletically, academically, and socially, something is still missing. My goal, as I share my heart with you, is to challenge you in your spiritual life. There are people who are pouring into you to become a developed athlete. You may have teachers or mentors challenging you academically. You may have friends for fellowship, growth, and socializing. But are you developing spiritually?

> *You need to try to grow in four ways: academically, athletically, socially, and spiritually.*

360-Degree Impact

Nearly 80 percent of NFL players severely struggle after they retire. They end up experiencing bankruptcy, divorce, or unemployment, and some even commit suicide. Avoiding these pitfalls requires a proper perspective on life. And when I entered the NFL, I didn't have it. But something changed the course of my life.

My first coach in the NFL was Chuck Noll. I was drafted to play for the Pittsburgh Steelers in 1977. The Steelers had won two Super Bowl championships by the time I joined the team, and in our very first team meeting, Coach Noll said something I had never even thought about. I walked into my first team meeting as an NFL player with my notebook and pen. I was ready to write down every word and capture the essence of what it would take to become a Super Bowl–winning NFL player. I was ready to pour my life into the NFL. What Coach Noll said, however, surprised me.

"For you new guys, welcome to the NFL," Coach Noll said. "But you need to understand that this is not your life's profession. Just because you get paid to do this doesn't mean this is your profession for life. Football is not life. Football is not *your* life. Part of my job is to help you get ready for your life's work."

I was stunned. I had just spent my whole life up to this point striving to get to the NFL, and this man was telling me that football is not my life's work. Fortunately, I was around Coach Noll for ten years, and I had the unique opportunity to understand what he really meant. I was also around a bunch of other guys who understood this truth as well. I learned early on in my NFL career that sports is a great "laboratory for life," but you have to keep it in perspective.

You see, most people around you have taken sports out of perspective and made it the "end all" of your life's focus. As a player, I believed it. I believed that all of my life's purposes would be fulfilled in the NFL. Too many parents get caught up in this mindset, thinking that their five-year-old or ten-year-old is on a path to make it into professional sports and somehow that goal is going to bring ultimate fulfillment. It's just not true.

But here's the real truth about sports straight from the NCAA. Over forty million kids play at least one organized team sport. We all agree that sports are great exercise, teamwork, and so forth. But, to be honest, your kid probably won't make it to the NFL. Of all high school varsity football players, less than 6 percent will go on to play college football, and that's even if you include Division III schools where scholarships are not allowed. Of the few who do play college football, less than 2 percent will get drafted into the NFL. The sobering statistics do not lie.

If you do make it to the professional level—though it's a great place to be—you will one day finish your career (and yes, you *will* finish) and wonder where your purpose in life has gone and what comes next. If sports was your purpose—and you finish at eighteen, at twenty-two, or even in your thirties—you are lost and have to start all over on a search for meaning.

This is the great truth that I received from Coach Noll. Football may be my profession for a temporary season of my life, but football is not my life profession, and more importantly, football is not my "purpose."

Thirty-five years later, Coach Noll is still influencing my life. That's why I love him, respect him, and feel like I was so blessed to play for him. He was certainly interested in developing us as great players, and he wanted to win football games. But he was far more interested in develop-ing us as people than developing us as play-ers. So take my advice and develop yourself as a person first and as a player second.

Photo courtesy of the Indianapolis Colts

I remember being in my thirties as an assistant coach and attending a coaches' conference in Texas. This was a high school coaches' conference, and there were eight thousand high school coaches there. After the meeting, I had coaches swamp me with questions about the "Cover 2 defense" and this play and that play. They were saying things like, "I don't teach in my school; I only coach, and I have to win. If I don't win games, I'm going to get fired." And this was *high school* football, in Texas (of course), thirty years ago! This is an example of what our country has done with sports. The idea that winning the Friday night football game is the most important thing in our city is a flaw in our value system. It's great to run out on the field prepared to bring a victory to our team and our community, but it's not the life-or-death situation our culture has made it out to be.

This is the reason we don't have enough coaches like Chuck Noll around anymore—because we don't reward the true value system as we should. Our culture rewards the coach who wins no matter what ... not the coach who does things the right way. Be a player or coach who values your development as a person more than your performance as a player. Be a jersey effect athlete.

The Super Bowl Isn't Everything

People ask me how I handled Super Bowl success, and you need to understand something. It was a great experience to coach the Indianapolis Colts and win Super Bowl XLI. But if you find yourself on the road to a Super Bowl someday, understand the mindset that I want to share with you. As much as I wanted our team to win that game, I understood the importance of keeping it in perspective. This wasn't a life-or-death moment. The sun was going to rise on Monday whether we won the game or lost it. We wanted to come in to the game prepared, and we wanted to do everything we could in our power to win the game. But we couldn't think of it as a life-or-death moment. We knew it would not shape our identities as people for the rest of our lives.

In Super Bowl XIII, the Steelers beat the Cowboys 35–31; it was Pittsburgh's third Super Bowl in five years. It was a thrilling game. But the first question from the media when we entered the locker room was not how we beat the Cowboys; it was not even about the game. The first question from the media was, "Do you think you can repeat?" As a player, I remember thinking, *Wow, it's just like Coach Noll taught us. We are at what I thought was the end of the journey. I thought this was the destination. But they want us to keep going. They want us to do more.* I wondered, *Where will it ever end? What is the ultimate goal? Where is the finish line?* As a young player, the Super Bowl experience taught me a big life lesson. If you get your identity caught up in an event like a Super Bowl, you are in for a tough fall. You can apply this to anyone. Maybe you're caught up in the hope of a promotion or job, or the hope of finding a spouse, or the hope of retirement. But the validation of who I am and where my identity comes from does not lie in a championship ring. My identity, my value, and the validation of me as a person come from my foundational relationship with God.

I'm telling you the truth. There is plenty of life beyond the world championship ring.

The Never-Ending Cycle of the World

The world validates its heroes by seeking to capture the moments in life where someone does something that's never been done before. I remember, as a coach, watching Peyton Manning's evolution and hearing what the world thought of him: *Here's a really talented guy, but he can't win the big game. He's done this or that, but he hasn't won a playoff game.*

So Peyton wins a playoff game … then they say, "Okay, he's won a playoff game, but he can't beat the Patriots."

So he beats the Patriots … then they say, "Well, he showed us something by beating the Patriots, but he still hasn't won a Super Bowl."

So he wins a Super Bowl … then they say, "He's going to go down as a great quarterback, but he's won only one Super Bowl with all that talent."

It just keeps going on and on and on.

If Peyton Manning won three Super Bowls, the world would say, "Peyton won three, but Joe Montana won four."

The world will always focus on the feats that have never been done before, but what is *really* important? These are the really important questions:

Who is Peyton Manning as a person?

What has he done to impact people's lives?

What impact has he had on his team and on professional sports?

But the world will always focus on comparisons; what we accomplish in sports is always compared to what someone else has done. It's a never-ending cycle, and it stands in a position to destroy you if you are not rooted in something bigger than wins and losses. If you allow the opinions of the world to define you, then you will always come up short, and you will live your life feeling that there was something else you should have done and that something else would have made it all complete. Let me tell you that it will never end! Don't let the world shape you. You'll end up empty.

Understand this about God: the thing that is so different about the way God validates a person is that God doesn't validate us by wins and losses. If you live your life as an athlete playing for his glory and giving your best for him, you will be validated by his approval and his acceptance. Your best is good enough for him, regardless of what the world measures in wins and losses. Your impact on the team, your impact on the lives of those around you, and your personal character as a person are a whole lot more important to God than the validation of this world. This is your jersey effect. And if your life is lived with a focus on God, you will not end up an empty shell.

What a Young Athlete Needs to Know About the Jersey Effect

Walk with me back into the locker room, and let's take a seat and talk.

The first piece of advice I want to give you comes from my favorite verse in the Bible, Matthew 16:26: "What good is it for a man to gain the whole world, yet forfeit his soul?" (NIV). As an athlete, you have the world in front of you. You can see the possibilities. You know you have the ability to do great things. So work hard and give your best, and see what you can do with the gifts God has given you … but *don't* pursue it at the expense of growing spiritually, and don't do it at the expense of being the person who God wants you to be.

The second piece of advice I would give you is this: you really have to look at yourself from God's standpoint and define yourself from

God's criteria. Seek to be a leader, not only athletically, but guide your teammates and others around you off the field as much as you would on the field. Don't just make a difference on the field, because at some point that's all going to be over.

What a College Athlete Needs to Know About the Jersey Effect

If there was one thing I would do different as a college athlete, I would go back and give more attention to my spiritual life while at the University of Minnesota. In my youth, I had parents who encouraged me spiritually, and in the NFL, I had the privilege to be around some great godly coaches and players who really encouraged me spiritually. But when I was in college, I kind of wasted four years of my walk with God. If there is one thing I regret, it's the realization later on in my life that I neglected my spiritual life as a college student. When I was a college athlete, my coach emphasized the importance of growing academically, athletically, and socially. But the piece that wasn't really emphasized was the spiritual dimension. I pretty much chose to focus on the other three areas of growth and ignore the spiritual areas of my life.

As a college student, my mind and heart were occupied with being a fantastic quarterback, winning a championship, and developing relationships that would get me into the NFL. And if there was any time left, I would grow spiritually. But here's the problem: there wasn't much time because I didn't make it a priority. College athletes today have even less time than I did with all the off-season training. So unless you really *make* time to grow spiritually, it can get away from you, and your spiritual growth will be stunted.

It's during this period of life when you are adjusting to your independence from your parents. Your parents aren't there to make sure you attend church, go to campus ministry Bible studies, and read your Bible on your own. It's now up to you to make those choices to grow spiritually. Your time will quickly get away from you if you aren't intentional about it. That's exactly what happened to me in college and again when I got to the NFL. Luckily, I met some guys who came to me and said, "Tony, this has got to be a priority in your life. And you'll see why it's important when you begin to see the challenges this lifestyle can bring upon you." I certainly did see the challenges the NFL lifestyle could bring; I saw some guys who handled it well, and I saw some guys who didn't handle it well. The guys who handled the challenges well were the guys who had a very, very strong Christian foundation.

Recently, I was asked to reflect on the greatest and happiest moments of my life. Without question, this is what came to mind:

It was in 1978, and I was at the Steelers' training camp sitting in a dorm room. Going into training camp, I had been diagnosed with

mononucleosis, so I wasn't allowed to practice. I was getting really frustrated, was afraid I was going to lose my job, and knew I was losing all of my conditioning, which I had worked hard for. My roommate was a guy named Donnie Shell. He sat me down and talked to me about what was going on in my life. It was during that talk that my eyes were opened, and I realized what was going on. My selfishness was stealing my happiness.

"Tony, you've professed that Christ is the most important thing

Photo courtesy of the Indianapolis Colts

in your life," Donnie said, "but I've noticed you over the last four or five weeks. You've felt like something may be happening with your football career, and for the first time in your life, you feel things aren't coming together as a football player. You're a mess. You say God is the most important thing in your life, but I think he's trying to find out if he really is."

We had a long and very frank discussion in the dorm room that day, and my eyes were opened. I realized that football had become more important than God. Getting onto the football field had become more important than being in the presence of God. Donnie read a number of verses from the Bible, and we examined my spiritual standpoint. That day, it hit me: if I am going to experience real peace and joy in my life, that joy is only going to come from my personal relationship with God. He has to be first in my life. And I decided that if God ever allowed me to play football again, I wasn't going to play for myself. I was going to play for him. I decided I would use the talents he gave me to glorify him, and if I didn't make the team, I'd still glorify him.

That moment in the training camp dorm room changed my life. The clarity and the peace that I came away with helped make me who I am today. It was what made the locker room experience after winning Super Bowl XLI with the Indianapolis Colts a very happy moment. It was what made the moment I was named head coach of the Tampa Bay Buccaneers so special. All those moments in my life that marked success were all the more special because I could keep them in perspective. *It's your profession, but it's not your life,* I'd tell myself. *Your purpose is much bigger than winning games and making money.*

I didn't sell my soul to my career in football. I placed God first, so whatever came my way—in the form of victory or defeat—was his, not mine. And that's a very happy place to be.

When You Lose

At the end of every competition, there is a winner, and there is a loser. My last game as an NFL coach with the Colts was a loss to the San Diego Chargers, a game we all thought we'd win en route to another Super Bowl.

The world thinks the only way God can use us is through victory and success. I remember my thoughts after winning Super Bowl XLI. I had seriously considered retiring. What a great time to go out—right after winning a Super Bowl! For two weeks after the Super Bowl I really thought I was going to retire.

But then I talked with Pastor Tony Evans, senior pastor of Oak Cliff Bible Fellowship and president of the Urban Alternative. Dr. Evans is a great spiritual leader, a great pastor, and a personal friend. He helped me understand a different perspective. You see, in the world's eyes, you can retire after a moment of success, and people remember your success, which can send a message that God's blessing is defined by success. But in God's eyes, it's not important that you end with a moment of success. If you read through the Bible, God didn't take people to heaven after their greatest victories. God didn't take David to heaven after he killed Goliath. But in the world's eyes, we desire to be remembered by a great victory. Because winning is glorified at a higher level by man than by God, we miss opportunities that God can use in our lives through defeat. You can have a great impact on people after a loss.

A lot of people over the years have come to me to express their appreciation for the way we handled winning the Super Bowl with the Colts. But I have had far more people come to me to share how they were inspired by the way I handled being fired by the Tampa Bay Buccaneers. The press conference comments I made after the Super Bowl with the Colts might have been interesting to some, but the press conference comments I made after being fired from the Buccaneers had a deeper impact on a lot of people.

On January 14, 2002, the Tampa Bay Buccaneers fired me. When I spoke to the press, I said, "It's been a great six years with Tampa Bay. When you're a Christian, you kind of look at things from a different perspective. Some things that are supposed to be bad, even though you're sad, they don't necessarily strike you as bad times."

You see, my strength and validation were in God, so during the trial I felt I could draw upon his strength and his plan for my future. I think that resonated with a lot of people. People can't necessarily relate to being an NFL coach, but they can relate to losing a job or circumstances that send their world into a tailspin. I'm not saying I didn't feel the pain of being fired, but I knew in my heart that God was in control, and the biggest thing in my life was not football, but God. That really helped.

People can really relate to adversity and defeat. Sports and life will bring a lot of failure, adversity, and defeat; don't be afraid to let the world see in you an example of how Christians handle defeat.

Purpose Beyond the Field

Players like Hunter Smith might not be headliners that come to everyone's mind in the Colts' success, but when you are on the inside, you truly understand the great impact players like Hunter have. I'm talking about the great impact on the team's success as well as the impact on the personal lives of teammates. When I was twenty-one years old, I was a rookie in an NFL locker room, and I wouldn't be the man I am today if it weren't for a few guys who reached out to me and gave direction to my life. I can think of a ton of guys on our Colts team that wouldn't be where they are today without Hunter Smith and his friendship and influence. To me, that kind of influence, spiritually, is much more important than a statistic like leading the league in punting or having 30 punts inside the 20-yard line as opposed to the 15.

Twenty years from now, having someone say thank you for having the kind of influence that changed his or her life is much more meaningful than having someone say thank you for that punt that landed on the 1-yard line.

What You'll Really Remember

The photo that was snapped in the locker room after the Super Bowl victory wasn't supposed to happen. We gathered to pray as a team, and I asked all the reporters to turn off their cameras. During the team prayer, one reporter snapped a picture anyway. That photo circulated around the world. God used it as a testimony of how we wanted our team to be remembered. Our desire was to stand up for God in moments of victory or defeat, speak up for God, and kneel before God when the cameras were off and no one was looking. Much has been said about that locker room photo, and God has used it greatly.

But for me, the more significant thing I take away from that team and season is not the Super Bowl victory, the media attention, or the hundred million people watching on TV. The thing I take away from that season is the reality that lives were changed that year. I'm talking about conversations I had with players in the locker room about their marriages or their spiritual lives. My greatest memories, even more than the Super Bowl, are the Friday afternoon Bible studies and the times God allowed me to encourage or counsel a player. That's what this life is about.

HUNTER REFLECTS

For me to come back and say *anything* after that would be like me, a third-string quarterback, telling Peyton Manning to modify his throwing technique. Ain't gonna happen. That's why this chapter is toward the end. All the books Tony has written—well, those aren't just empty words on a page. He's written them with his life. The way you picture Tony is exactly the way he is. He is what you get. Tony's *life* encapsulates the jersey effect more than anyone I know. And what he just wrote captures the jersey effect perfectly, specifically in athletics. He's dealt with all of it.

I really appreciated Tony's willingness, in collaboration with this book, to share his personal struggles while he was a young quarterback at the University of Minnesota and a defensive back with the Pittsburgh Steelers. Who would have thought that Tony Dungy neglected his spiritual development as a collegiate player? Who would have thought that Donnie Shell would have to sit Tony down and tell him that he wasn't living like Christ was the center of this life? I respect Tony Dungy. But many Christians put him on a pedestal. I'm thankful he shared some of his personal struggles while he was a young athlete. That's what is so great about Tony. He's willing to be transparent. At the end of the day, Tony Dungy is just a man—an influential man—but still just a man. But I've never had another coach like him.

When Tony was hired by the Colts, I saw the news on television (as players, we didn't even get a call first). I remember saying, "Of all the guys out there, *he's* the guy I want to play for." Six years later, he was standing in front of fifty-four thousand Colts fans at the RCA Dome celebrating a Super Bowl victory when we arrived home from Miami.

I'll never forget what he said when he stepped up to the podium: "When Jim Irsay called me five years ago, he told me, 'I want you to be our coach and help us win the Super Bowl.' He told me, 'We are going win it the right way. We are going to win it with great guys; win it with class and dignity. We are going to win it in a way that will make Indianapolis proud.'"

Tony won the right way. He treated his players like men, dealt with his coaches rationally, had an impact on the lives of his staff and the guys in the locker room, and was also effective on the field. He didn't just see his players and staff as important men who could help him win a Super Bowl. He saw their value. They weren't just football players. They were men with souls who were all striving for something to fulfill and satisfy. Tony was the best coach I ever played for and one of the greatest men I'll ever know. I'm sure of it. Tony taught me that my life is not defined by football, but it's all about the impact I could make when I was willing to wear my jersey in the proper perspective. What Chuck Noll was for Tony, Tony was for me. Without that 360-degree influence of the jersey effect, I wouldn't understand it like I do today.

Tony taught me that my life is not defined by football, but it's all about the impact I could make when I was willing to wear my jersey in the proper perspective.

I only had one scare with Tony during my entire career with the Colts. It had to do with his son, Eric. Eric was eight at the time, and we had a cool friendship ... or so I thought. He would always come to practice, toss me the football on the sideline, and hang out with some of us on the team.

One day, we were tossing the football to one another before practice. *Tossing.* You know, like underhand. Well, when I flipped it to him from five yards away, the football apparently jammed his finger. Eric was only eight, and he dropped to the ground, writhing in pain. *Oh no!* I said to myself. *I just maimed Tony Dungy's son.*

The next thing I knew, Eric was running over to tell his dad. I couldn't believe it ... the little booger was tattling on me. I remember walking up to Tony and saying, "Hey, Coach, I didn't mean to hurt your son, and I'm sorry. We were just tossing the—"

"Hunter," Tony said, smiling and holding his hand up. "He's a little dramatic at this age."

Now, of course, Eric is a receiver at Oregon. And he's a lot tougher physically and mentally. But that was the most scared I ever was of Tony Dungy.

Sorry if you wanted something deep in my reflection. But you just read a whole chapter written by a best-selling author. Not gonna find me instructing Peyton Manning on the sideline. That's my only insight.

THE SNAP

That's what was eerie about the whole ordeal—looking back and realizing that *this* was how it ended.

It began on the one-thousand-acre cattle ranch, where my brother would shove my face in the dirt every time I dropped a pass and where my father and I would throw the pigskin in the yard for hours on end—then to playing quarterback at Sherman High School in the football-consumed state of Texas—then to punting at Notre Dame, a school with one of the richest football histories in the NCAA—then to the Colts, where I was a part of the most successful organizational decade in the history of the NFL. Overall, my football career was a cauldron of memories and achievements—especially for a punter—yet *this* was how it ended.

Closing Out the Colts

Two years earlier, in the 2008/09 season, something else came to an end: my time with the Colts. It was two seasons after we won the Super Bowl, and we were on pace to do it again. We were better than the year before when we lost to the Chargers in the playoffs, and we had the Super Bowl monkey off our backs. We were going to win another Super Bowl, and we all knew it.

But San Diego stunned us in the wild-card game, defeating us 23–17. In the fourth quarter, I remember taking the field, having to punt deep from our own end zone. I was nervous. The game was close, and we still had a legitimate shot of winning. But it depended on the punt. That far

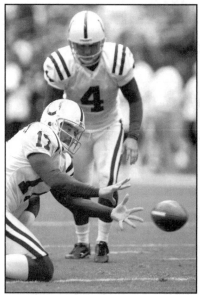

Photo courtesy of the Indianapolis Colts

back, the Chargers could easily block it or force a turnover, then score a quick touchdown, and put the game out of reach.

Justin Snow snapped me the ball; I grabbed it, took one step, and booted a 63-yard punt down the field. Our coverage unit made the tackle, and as I walked off the field, I realized something. If we didn't make a comeback, it might be my last punt as an Indianapolis Colt.

After the game, when the 8–8 Chargers were walking off the field with an overtime victory, leaving us behind as we hung our heads, I looked at Jeff Saturday. Nothing about it felt right. We were locked and loaded, ready to play three more games. We knew this would probably be Tony's last season, and we just felt like we were going to win another Super Bowl for him. But our dreams came crashing down. And as I stared at Jeff, it hit me. We were both playing out our contract that year, and one of us would probably be gone come next season, and it was most likely going to be me. Remember, Peyton needed a center, not a punter.

"Brother," I said, looking at Jeff. "Will you walk off the field with me one more time?"

Jeff knew what I was alluding to. After arriving in Indianapolis together as rookies—he, a hippie boy who went undrafted out of college, and I, a country kid from Texas, neither of us ever dreaming we'd stay in Indy together for ten years—our time together had finally expired.

He looked at me and said, "Hunter, it would be a pleasure."

At that moment, someone took our picture; it is my favorite photograph from my NFL career. As Jeff and I walked off the field with our arms around each other, Matt Giordano was kneeling in front of us, praying. I didn't know it until I saw the photo. But it was a perfect picture of the brotherhood we had in Indianapolis, a bond that was based on Christ and love.

I ended up being right. It was my last game as a Colt. It wasn't a bad way to go out, per se. I had played out my contract, and honestly, I was surprised they kept me around that long to begin with. After all, I was on the same team as Peyton Manning, which meant I only punted fifty times a year. And even when I did punt, it was usually from midfield, not deep in our own territory. I was making a good amount of money, not top five in the league, but on the upper end of punters. Yet still, they kept me around for ten years.

In 2008, our special teams coach tried to convince Colts President Bill Polian to keep me. But financially, it wasn't realistic. I was coming off of my best season statistically, and the Colts were trying to save some money where they could save money and go cheaper across the spectrum. Another thing that didn't help was that the NFL was already preparing for the lockout and trying to cut costs wherever they could. So where do you make cuts? You make them at my position.

I'll always remember my last day at the Colts' complex. I hadn't been officially released yet, but I knew it was coming. There was an overwhelming sense in my spirit and in the tone of the higher-ups that I wouldn't be a Colt the following season. So I worked out, showered, and then went from office to office to say my good-byes.

First, I went to Bill Polian's office. He was a crafty businessman. It's tough to be a general manager in the NFL without hurting people, but he drafted me, and that was special. I remember breaking down, crying, and telling him, "I'm leaving here without any bitterness toward you.

I'm not angry. I'm not disgruntled. I'm thankful for everything you've done for me, and I'm thankful that you drafted me." Moved and tearing up as well, he told me he loved me and gave me a hug.

Next I went to Coach Caldwell's office because I wanted to tell him good-bye and because I wanted to gauge the chances of me staying. But he repeated my farewell and didn't offer any kind of indication that the Colts were going to make a move to keep me. I talked to a few more of the coaches; but because it was the offseason and the day before free agency, there weren't many players around.

Perhaps the hardest good-byes were to the maintenance workers at the Colts complex, like Doug Melton (the mail guy who wore a million other hats), Troy Glendenning (who handled the fields), Scott Davis,

John Scott, and Angel, Frog, T, and Smack (and no, those weren't their real names). If you think about it, I probably played with five hundred different players during my decade in Indianapolis. But the workers at the Colts complex were

Photo courtesy of the Indianapolis Colts

always there. Though I knew some of my teammates would be gone the next year, I knew Doug Melton, a reformed drug addict who was now following God, would always be by my side. They were some of my closest friends, and I talked to them nearly every single day for a decade.

The last thing I did was clean out my locker. It was an emotional and nostalgic moment, as God allowed me to be alone to reflect on what he'd given me. As I opened the bottom compartment, the culmination of ten memorable years in Indianapolis began to catch up to me. Most people emptied their lockers every year because they knew they may not be back. Not me. Year after year, I knew the Colts would keep me. This was home. Going through my locker was like diving into my own personal time capsule. I found my favorite kicking shoe from five years back, the Adidas Gerd Müller. I found sideline hats from every season. And I even found my Super Bowl cleats with confetti still stuck to them. It was like looking at the rings on a tree trunk.

I packed my belongings, stared at my empty locker, and took down my name tag. My time in Indianapolis was done.

"Deserts of Virginia"

I was at the prime of my career.

Thirty-one years old.

Coming off my best season, statistically.

Looking for a big-time contract.

And there were four teams after me: the Titans, Saints, Packers, and Redskins. It was soon narrowed down to Green Bay and Washington. It was a hard decision, but I went with the Redskins.

My first season with the Redskins (2009), I hurt my groin a few games in and wrestled with it all season long. There was one positive, though; I became the first special teams player in NFL history to throw *and* rush for a touchdown in the same season—an 8-yard touchdown run off a fake field goal in week 1 against the New York Giants and a 35-yard touchdown pass to fullback Mike Sellers in week 10. We finished 4–12 that year as the Colts won their first fourteen games in Jim Caldwell's first season and lost to the Saints in the Super Bowl. The Redskins signed me again four games into the 2010 season after Josh Bidwell got hurt, and I punted for three games. By that time, I was already beginning to reflect on my career. Darrin Gray and I had begun to write *The Jersey Effect*, and as we wrote each week, we were wrestling with the truths and the lies of my NFL experience. I was struggling more than I expected in Washington. That year, the Packers went on to win the Super Bowl, which was strange because I turned down a three-year deal with them and would have been a two-time Super Bowl champion. And of course, the year before, the Colts almost won a Super Bowl.

If I'm being honest, it was difficult to be on a team that was abysmal, especially after my tenure with the Colts. On top of that, it was a difficult environment. Washington, DC, is one of the most disconnected places in the world. Hardly anyone who lives in Washington is from Washington. There wasn't the same intimacy that Indiana had. Plus, I was injured both years, and they were trying to get rid of me. Virginia was beautiful, with the towering mountains and winding roads. But it felt like a desert.

There, as Jen and I were both struggling with a difficult transition period, I wrote this love song called "Deserts of Virginia." This is the original version and one of my wife's favorites.

They said ya gotta move on
They said ya gotta leave this place
They said it's all over
They're gonna find a younger face

This is what they promised
This is just what they do
We can say they warned us
And for once they told the truth.

But I will not be afraid
That life has turned this way

Because the deserts of Virginia ain't so dry
With the way that you look at me tonight
And the mountains here before us ain't so high
When I'm holding onto you for the climb

So baby put your arms inside of mine
In the deserts of Virginia tonight.

What about the future?
What about dates and times?

What about the culture?
What if it passes us by?
What if there's a fallout?
What if we're all we have?
Here with our Maker
And the clothes on our backs

I will not be afraid
There on that day

Because the deserts of Virginia ain't so dry
With the way that you look at me tonight
And the mountains here before us ain't so high
When I'm holding on to you for the climb

So baby fall into these arms of mine
In the deserts of Virginia tonight

The Snap

It felt like every single fan in that 66,124-person Redskins crowd was glaring at me as I walked off that muddy field in shame. It was Sunday, December 12, 2010, and week 14. We had just lost to the Tampa Bay Buccaneers, 17–16, pretty much extinguishing our slim playoff hopes.

We had a 10–3 lead at halftime, but the Bucs held us scoreless for most of the second half. They had a 17–10 advantage as our quarterback, Donovan McNabb, and our offense tried to march down the field. With nine seconds left in the game, McNabb threw a 6-yard pass to Santana Moss for a touchdown to make the score 17–16 in favor of the Buccaneers. We set up for the extra point to tie the game and send it into overtime. My job was to catch the snap and place the ball for our kicker to punch in the extra point … just like I'd done for the last dozen years. I didn't even think about it anymore. It was so routine. The only thing I was usually thinking about was getting back to the sidelines.

The snap, however, was high, the ball was wet, and I dropped it. It bounced clumsily off my hands, and the Buccaneers recovered the ball and ran out the clock for a 17–16 victory. I felt like I was standing naked on FedEx Field. I was a disgrace. And it was all my fault. I dropped the snap on an extra point that would've sent the game into overtime. As I walked off the field, I didn't know that it was the end—that a dropped snap would be the final play of my otherwise successful career—but it was. I was a twelve-year NFL veteran. This was what I did, game in and game out. If there was one thing I could do, it was this: catch the ball.

Yet *this* was how it ended … on a dropped snap.

I hit the shower, and it was as if God began to stir my heart in a new way. I knew I had a decision to make. Yes, the snap was high. Yes, the ball was wet. Yes, our kicker missed two field goals in that game, a 34-yarder and a 24-yarder. And yes, our offense had first-and-goals from the 8-, 6-, 5-, and 2-yard lines and only scored two touchdowns. But it didn't matter. I wasn't concerned with shifting the blame, defending myself, or elevating my past success. I was concerned with my jersey. How was my jersey effect going to be remembered in the face of adversity and defeat? I sensed that God was saying that this was an opportunity to face the press and not do what I might normally do. This is a word-for-word transcript of what I told the media after the game:

> In the NFL, when something catastrophic like this happens on the last play, everybody says, "Well, you know, what about the dropped pass earlier in the game? What about the missed holding call? What about the bad pass? What about the missed field goals? What about? What about? What about?" But at the end, when you have an opportunity to tie it up and the whole game comes down to that, we did all we could to be in the game, and it's all my fault. I have a beautiful wife, and I have three

How was my Jersey Effect going to be remembered in the face of adversity and defeat?

wonderful children, and I have a faithful God, and that is reality to me. It's not ideology, and it's not a fairy tale. It's not that this just doesn't mean anything to me, because it is a letdown to the organization, but I can move forward and play Dallas because my reality is maybe a little bit different.

My ultimate hope is in him, it's not in this game. It's never going to be in this game. My life is in his hands. God is my reality. I'm not saying the game doesn't matter. Of course it matters. People's livelihoods are on the line when athletes don't perform well. But ultimately, my life is in God's hands, and his purposes are more important in my life than anything else.

As absurd as it sounds, winning the Super Bowl and dropping a snap in front of sixty-six thousand people had a similar feel. They were both windows into the soul. In both instances, the world betrayed me. The veil was pulled away, and I could see the world for what it really was.

Photo courtesy of the Indianapolis Colts

It's not fulfilling. It's not rewarding. It's empty. But on the other side of that horrible experience, God was still there, and he was the same. God was *for* me.

I was "important" as a football player. When we won the Super Bowl, I was important because we brought the coveted Vince Lombardi Trophy to Indianapolis and brought joy to people's lives. In a way, when I dropped the snap, I was still important because I lost the Redskins the game and brought frustration into fans and teammates' lives. Importance, you see, isn't always a good thing. All importance means is having significance—good or bad. And if your life is built around importance, you'll live a life replete with roller-coaster circumstances and inconsistent emotions. Dropping that snap was frustrating, of course, but because I understood my value as a person—that my identity was in Christ—I knew I'd be fine. I was still valuable. I was still loved by the source of love.

The truth is God exists outside of our consequences, our goals, and our outcomes. So God brought me to a place to ask myself, "Are you willing to have your dreams shattered? Are you willing to fail at what you do best if it brings God glory? Does he mean enough to you to allow him to use defeat in your life for his own glory?"

In the midst of that moment of defeat, God impressed on my heart that my jersey as an athlete is to be used for his glory, not only in victory but also in moments of defeat. And he will be glorified in me if my reality is in him and not contingent upon his giving me all I want in areas of success.

After my statement to the press, Alex Parker, a reporter for WJLA-TV in Washington, DC, came up to me and said, "Hunter, that was the greatest four-minute interview I have experienced in covering sports." That surprised me because all I did was tell the truth.

On December 14, two days after the game against Tampa Bay, I was released from the Washington Redskins, and it struck me: that snap may have been my last offering to the game of football. Did I mention that the world betrays you?

I paused to remember that God gave me the incredible opportunity to use my jersey for the Lord in the biggest game of my life, the Super Bowl with the Indianapolis Colts. We stood up for God and gave him glory, and we knelt down before the Lord in the privacy of the locker room, away from the crowds.

But what happened on December 12, 2010, on FedEx Field in Washington, DC, was a new lesson on using my jersey effect for God. I had the opportunity to decide if my commitment to God, and listening to his voice and choosing to follow his lead, was more important than my reputation, more important than my own success, and more important than football. I chose to listen to him. And no surprise, the impact of that decision to lay down my life for him in a moment of defeat has had more of an influence than other times in my life, when I chose to give God glory in moments of victory.

Three questions stuck in my heart that day as I walked off the field, having been the reason we lost the game. I wondered if, as an athlete, I was willing to (1) stand up for God in moments of victory, (2) kneel before God in private and acknowledge it is him who deserves the praise,

and (3) lay down my life before him in moments of defeat and allow him to use the trials of life for his own glory.

It was worth it. And as crazy as it sounds, I wouldn't go back again and catch that ball, even if I

Photo courtesy of the Indianapolis Colts

could. It was a horrible experience—no doubt—but I wouldn't change a thing. It gave me an opportunity to use my jersey. Romans 8:28 says, "And we know that in all things God works for the good of those who love him, who have been called according to his purpose" (NLT). The good that God can bring from our trial is enhanced by our response to the trial.

There were at least twenty-eight news articles written within forty-eight hours of my release from the Redskins. So much of what was written was speaking to the personal responsibility I took for that last game and the response I gave to the press. I wasn't trying to "fall on my sword" or be known as noble. I was just trying to look at this from an eternal perspective. How could I return to an NFL reunion in ten years and be known as the guy who cast blame on his teammates? How could I proclaim my faith for so many years and then not own up to my mistakes and come across as self-centered and egocentric? No, at that moment in time, a dropped snap was my cross to bear.

Whether it was my talking about the Super Bowl at the beginning of the book or the dropped snap at the end of book, God called me to use my jersey for his glory, no matter the circumstance. God calls you to do the same with your jersey—whether you're a businessman, a mother, a plumber, or an athlete. You have a choice. Because with every jersey comes power—power to destroy and power to influence. And unfortunately, in the NFL, it destroys 78 percent of the players (and it *tries* to destroy 100 percent of them). It will destroy you, too … if you let it. You learned that from Jeff Saturday, whose jersey tried to make him selfish; from Ben Utecht, whose jersey distracted him and shook his foundation; from Dylan Gandy, whose jersey turned football into an idol that dictated his moods; from Matt Giordano, whose jersey made him shy away from sharing the gospel; from Tarik Glenn, whose jersey challenged his identity in Christ; and from Justin Snow, whose jersey led him down a popular path of sin in the NFL. You learned how to prevent the jersey from hijacking your faith from Jim Caldwell, who lives a life with prayer at the foundation; from Reggie Hodges, whose trials magnified his ministry and encouraged us to embrace the Lord at all times, good and bad; from Clyde Christensen, who has a passion for fellowship; from Tony Dungy, who stressed growth in four areas (academic, athletic, social, and spiritual); and from all of the players who turned away from the enslaving ways of the jersey to pursue Christ.

The impetus for this book came all the way back in 1993, when I heard a message that changed my life. The message came from former Baltimore Colts player Willie Franklin, and at seventeen years old, I was captivated. Captivated that I was witnessing a bold and mighty man of God. Captivated that I was witnessing an athlete who was in love with Christ. Captivated that he was making an impact *after* his playing career was over.

I spoke to him recently on the phone, the first time we've spoken since that summer of 1993 at church camp. One of the last things he told me before I hung up was this: "Hunter, we're all just stones that are thrown into a spiritual pond … and you don't know how far the ripples will go."

I had already started working on this book when I sat in the locker room at FedEx Field, waiting for the media to arrive at my locker. But in that moment, I knew I had a chance to live out the purpose of this book. I had a chance to back up what I believe with action. It's easy to give glory to God after winning a Super Bowl, to kneel after a victory, or to point to the sky after a touchdown. But what do you do after a game-changing gaffe? What do you do when you haven't won a game all season? When you're cut seven times? When your son dies unexpectedly? When this world betrays you with a kiss?

This is what you do. You allow God to use you. You allow God to pick you up and cast you into a spiritual pond. You allow God to make an impact—an impression—as you make a splash on the surface of the water. You allow God to make you *sink*.

And then you watch the ripples above … the ripples from the jersey.

AUTHOR BIOGRAPHIES

HUNTER SMITH is a unique blend of performing artist and professional athlete. He's a committed Christian, twelve-year NFL veteran, Super Bowl champion, public speaker, worship leader, Billboard top twenty Christian adult contemporary artist, singer/songwriter of The Hunter Smith Band, renowned storyteller, and most recently author of *The Jersey Effect*, a book designed to teach important life lessons to athletes, coaches, and parents about how to keep sports in proper perspective.

Photo courtesy of the Indianapolis Colts

He was a multisport standout from Sherman High School and two-time Texas All-State selection in football. Coming out of high school he was highly recruited and chose the University of Notre Dame, where he played multiple positions for head coach Lou Holtz. Hunter punted every game of his four-year career and graduated in 1999 with a degree in theology and sociology.

Hunter was drafted by and played for the Indianapolis Colts for ten seasons, during which he received many honors, including being named to the NFL All-Rookie Team and three-time alternate to the Pro Bowl.

The Colts franchise recorded the most wins of any team in NFL history over the span of a decade under the leadership of Tony Dungy, Hunter's greatest sports role model, including winning Super Bowl XLI to cap off the 2006 season. Hunter signed as a free agent with the Washington Redskins in 2009, where he played for two seasons. During his tenure with Washington, he rushed for a touchdown against the New York Giants and passed for a 35-yard touchdown against the Denver Broncos, becoming the only special teams player in NFL history to both run and pass for a touchdown in the same season. He officially retired from professional football in 2011. Hunter serves as director of the Sports and Culture Initiative at the Sagamore Institute, a national think tank based in Indianapolis.

Hunter captivates audiences with a powerful message that is full of humbling and humorous experiences. He is enthusiastic about exposing people to God's truth and the world's lies. Hunter has carried his message on national and international stages through his gifts of speaking and singing. Hunter is a professional songwriter and guitarist and is the lead singer for The Hunter Smith Band, which released a new album in April of 2012. He and his wife, Jennifer, reside in Zionsville, Indiana, with their three children, Josiah, Samuel, and Lydia.

DARRIN GRAY has a unique window into the National Football League by virtue of his day-to-day involvement with All Pro Dad, Family First's national fatherhood program cofounded by Tony Dungy and Clyde Christensen. Darrin interacts with NFL athletes, coaches, and alumni who serve as spokesmen for All Pro Dad, and he has conducted programming with over half of the NFL franchises. He develops innovative partnership strategies to reach families via special events, broadcast, and new media with the assistance of media partners and corporate sponsors.

He conceptualized *The Jersey Effect* years ago when he wondered what motivated some athletes like Tony Dungy to use their professional platform in sports, their jersey, to make a positive impact both on and off the field. A few years later he invited NFL punter Hunter Smith, while he was still playing in the NFL, to coauthor the book and to help him explore the many ways that sports shape culture, with the help of his world champion teammates and coaches.

Photo courtesy of the Indianapolis Colts

Darrin began his journey with teams in the midnineties when he worked with all of the notable professional and amateur sports organizations on behalf of the *Indianapolis Star*, where he worked from 1992 to 2004. As general sales manager he directed a large staff responsible for $40 million in annual revenue across multiple divisions: national advertising, sports marketing, and events marketing. In 2004, he became CEO of Brandirect, a corporate brand and communications consultancy that served many notable sports organizations, including the Indianapolis Colts.

He serves on several not-for-profit boards: National Association of Christian Athletes, Greater Indianapolis Chamber of Commerce, and Central Indiana Better Business Bureau. He is a passionate public speaker who enjoys inspiring audiences to reach their ultimate potential on topics that include strategic sports philanthropy, faith, family, and fatherhood.

Darrin graduated with honors in 1989 with a degree in theology from Hanover College. He volunteers as chaplain for the Home School Lions High School and Middle School football teams. He and his wife of seventeen years, Leslie, reside in Fishers, Indiana, and have three children.

STEPHEN COPELAND is an up-and-coming staff writer and columnist at *Sports Spectrum* magazine, a national Christian sports publication that has been around for twenty-eight years.

He graduated from Grace College in Winona Lake, Indiana, where he served as sports information director with his best friend, Josh Neuhart, and worked under his mentor, Chad Briscoe. Stephen played four years of varsity golf at Grace and graduated with a degree in journalism and Bible. He is from Plainfield, Indiana, and is the son of Kim and Mark Copeland; he now resides in North Carolina.

KEN TURNER serves as chaplain of the National Association of Christian Athletes (NACA) and assistant director of Fort Bluff Camp.

He has been in full-time youth ministry for twenty-five years and has devoted his life to impacting youth and families, having served as a youth pastor in Nashville, Tennessee; South Bend, Indiana; and Indianapolis, Indiana. Ken is the author of *High Impact Teen*, a one-year spiritual guidebook used by thousands of teenagers in the United States and overseas. In 2008, Ken formed an outreach ministry to reach troubled youth, raised financial support, and went into the inner city and correctional facilities of Indianapolis to reach teens whom no one else could. Through this ministry, hundreds of youth have come to Christ. Ken lives in the mountains of Tennessee with his wife, Jennifer, and their three children, Bethany, Jillian, and Brett.

high
impact teen

www.highimpactteens.org

Photo courtesy of the Indianapolis Colts